A COMMON TABLE

80 RECIPES and STORIES from MY SHARED CULTURES

CYNTHIA CHEN
McTERNAN

Creator of *Two Red Bowls*

RODALE.

Copyright © 2018 by Cynthia Chen McTernan
All rights reserved.

Published in the United States by Rodale Books,
an imprint of the Crown Publishing Group, a division
of Penguin Random House LLC, New York.
crownpublishing.com
rodalebooks.com

RODALE and the Plant colophon are registered trademarks
of Penguin Random House LLC.

Library of Congress Cataloging-in-Publication Data
is available upon request.

ISBN 978-1-63565-002-0
Ebook ISBN 978-1-63565-003-7

Printed in China

Cover and interior design by Rae Ann Spitzenberger
Cover and interior photographs by Cynthia Chen McTernan

10 9 8 7 6 5 4 3 2 1

First Edition

*For Andrew
and Luke*

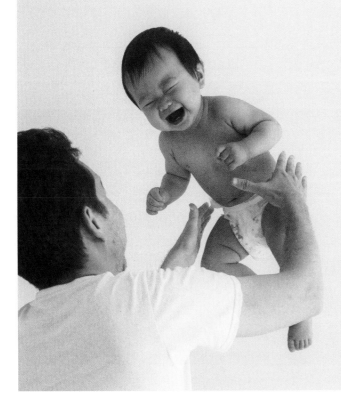

CONTENTS

CELEBRATIONS & GATHERINGS

ON THE SIDE

INTRODUCTION

Around the time that I first began thinking about this book, my husband, Andrew, and I were in the middle of a cross-country move from Brooklyn, New York, to Los Angeles, California. We were junior attorneys partway through our third years at law firms in Manhattan, expecting our first baby, and, with our little guy on the way, trying to figure out where it was that we wanted him to arrive.

I grew up in Greenville, South Carolina, a city big enough for an airport but small enough that the airport only had two terminals, friendly and slow-moving and comfortable. After going to college three hours away in North Carolina, I trekked north to snowy Cambridge, Massachusetts, for law school, which led to my first gainful employment as an attorney in New York. In the five-and-a-half frigid winters since I'd left the Carolinas, my family had moved to Southern California; my husband's family, by turn, had always been in Hawaii. Neither of them were very close to New York. Even though we'd never spent more than a week in California, we decided to move to Los Angeles for family—because we wanted to live closer to our siblings and parents, and because we hoped sunny LA would be where the story of our own family began. (Of course, the warm weather didn't hurt.)

So, when I was about four months pregnant, an apartment in a little duplex on the west side of LA became our home. It was bright and airy and filled to the brim with California sunshine. We started that thing called "nesting," fawning over (and then cursing while assembling) cribs and baby swings. With five months to go until our son arrived, we talked endlessly about what life would be like with him. What did we want to pass down to him? What would being a family mean for us, and for him? And—because for me, it always comes back to food—what would he eat?

A few months later Luke arrived, and with him the answers to our questions. Family meant hazy early mornings, bleary-eyed midnight diaper changes, and sunny Saturday afternoons crawling around on all fours. It meant visits from his Chinese grandparents on my side of the family, with stuffed monkeys for his Chinese zodiac year in tow, and, on my husband's side, weekly Skype sessions with Luke's Irish grandpa and his Korean *halmuni* in Honolulu, who dove into planning Luke's first birthday party, his *dol,* with gusto. Our baby's first purées were *jook* (or congee, page 24, depending on who you ask!), the purple sweet potato familiar to my Hawaii-born husband, the bright orange yam familiar to me; his first finger foods were my mother's soy-glazed salmon (page 118) and little bites of pork and vegetable dumplings (page 157).

Over the course of his first year, I came to realize that, in many ways, Luke embodied the spirit of the book I wanted to write. He is, after all, a combination of "shared cultures." His mom is a Chinese girl who grew up in South Carolina, eating *mapo tofu* alongside cornbread (page 213) and washing it down with sweet tea. His dad is a Korean-Irish boy who grew up halfway around the world in Hawaii, toting Spam *musubi* (page 87) to school and coming home to kimchi fried rice (page 113). In my little guy, I see a mix of cultures that is both incredibly diverse and utterly American. And those cultures, the food he eats, the traditions we're building together with him, all have so much more in common than first meets the eye.

As I wrote this book over the course of Luke's first year, *A Common Table* became a chronicle of all of these things. These recipes are a journal of the food that I make for our little family, reflecting the myriad cultures and influences that make us who we are. There are Chinese dishes that my mother taught me when I first moved away from home and, missing her cooking terribly, emailed and called her incessantly to learn how to make her spicy braised lamb (page 164) and Ginger Shrimp & Green Peas (page 191), thousands of miles away from home. Alongside those are recipes from the American South, pimento cheese (page 207) and flaky biscuits (page 52), food that makes me nostalgic for my childhood and the baking-hot summers of South Carolina, and the Sweet Tea (page 258) that accompanied every meal growing up.

And then there are the Korean dishes that my husband introduced to me when we began dating as law students in Boston, and that I later learned to cook from my mother-in-law, peering over her shoulder in

THESE RECIPES
ARE A JOURNAL
OF THE FOOD THAT
I MAKE FOR OUR
LITTLE FAMILY,
REFLECTING THE
MYRIAD CULTURES
AND INFLUENCES
THAT MAKE US
WHO WE ARE.

her apartment in downtown Honolulu. You can also find a few home-made takes on the Hawaii staples that my husband misses most when he's on the mainland, cobbled together from my trials and his taste-tests until they reminded him most of home.

Importantly, putting all these recipes in one place revealed that they had far more in common than I'd realized—for instance, that the dumplings in kimchi *sujebi* (page 82) are the same as the flat dumplings in familiar Southern chicken and dumplings (see page 79), and even the same as the wrappers for the Potstickers (page 157) that I ate when I was a child, or that *char siu* pork (page 76), traditionally roasted on hooks, can be made just as easily in the oven as baby-back ribs can, even though they are traditionally smoked.

Finally, sprinkled between these are recipes that don't fit neatly within any of these categories. There are recipes for foods we've loved in places we've traveled and that I've sought to re-create at home. Matcha-Glazed Swirl Bread (page 232) that we had in a basement food hall in Japan on our honeymoon, for instance, or soft, savory ham and egg buns (page 35) that I loved while studying abroad in Hong Kong. There are playful explorations of all of the above, dishes that are a little bit uncon-ventional but still so familiar, like Milk Tea Rice Pudding (page 248) or Sweet Sesame Skillet Cornbread (page 213). If the traditional dishes in this book represent where we come from—my family, my husband's family, and the traditions that were passed down to us—I like to think of these "new" dishes as the quirky emblem of where we are going.

Ultimately, I wrote *A Common Table* because I know food can bridge all kinds of distances, geographical or cultural, to bring us all around the same table. It represents the traditions and loved ones from our past and present, and it can represent things that are totally new to us, too. Food is what connects us, a common denominator that sustains all of us, both physically and emotionally—and I hope this book will serve to make that only more true.

FOOD CAN BRIDGE ALL KINDS OF DISTANCES, GEOGRAPHICAL OR CULTURAL, TO BRING US ALL AROUND THE SAME TABLE.

NOTES ON INGREDIENTS
& EQUIPMENT

This cookbook is meant to be a repertoire of all the foods that have made my little household what it is—the ones that make us the happiest, that have gotten my family through the late nights, that remind us of the places we've been. In other words, they are the ones we really eat day to day. So I tried hard not to include any ingredients or equipment that might not be readily accessible, because I'm hoping some of these recipes will become your day-to-day choices, too. Still, there are a few things that simply make our most-loved foods what they are, but which might be hard to come by. For these ingredients, I've included at least two or three recipes that incorporate them, so that nothing is single-purpose. Where possible, there are also notes regarding possible substitutes and online resources.

Ingredients

CHINKIANG (BLACK) VINEGAR. Something like a Chinese equivalent to balsamic vinegar, Chinkiang vinegar is dark and pungent, with a complex flavor derived from rice and malt, among other things. I most often use *Koon Chun* brand, which is available both online and in Chinese supermarkets.

FISH SAUCE. Many Korean dishes, especially broths and soups, incorporate a touch of dried anchovy or fish sauce into their base to lace the dish with an extra complex, savory, umami undercurrent. (In Chinese cuisine, dried shrimp often serves the same purpose.) I prefer fish sauce over dried anchovy, as I find it increasingly accessible in most supermarkets. I like *Three Crabs*, though I have found that most any brand will do—you may simply need to adjust the amount of fish sauce you use depending on the particular brand.

KIMCHI. At this point, this fiery-red, spicy, fermented cabbage practically needs no introduction. However, the quality of store-bought kimchi does vary quite a bit, which in turn will heavily affect the flavor of dishes in which it is used. Most brands available in Korean supermarkets will be decent if you can get to one; you can also try asking a restaurant that has kimchi that you like whether they sell it in bulk or if they have recommendations for where to buy it.

KOREAN CHILI PASTE (*GOCHUJANG*). Spicy, but with a distinct sweetness and smokiness, *gochujang* is a fermented chili paste that adds a uniquely Korean heat to spicy dishes. If you're at a well-stocked Korean market, you'll find they sell different spice levels—I most often use *CJ Haechandle* brand, medium spicy.

KOREAN CHILI POWDER (*GOCHUGARU*). Made from crushed sun-dried Korean chili peppers, *gochugaru* is a smoky red pepper powder used to make kimchi, and can be added to sauces for a little heat. Any brand you find on Amazon or in a Korean supermarket should work just fine.

MATCHA. Matcha is a type of Japanese tea made from dried green tea leaves that have been crushed finely into a verdant, fragrant powder. It has a long and rich history at the center of traditional Japanese tea ceremonies, but its powdered

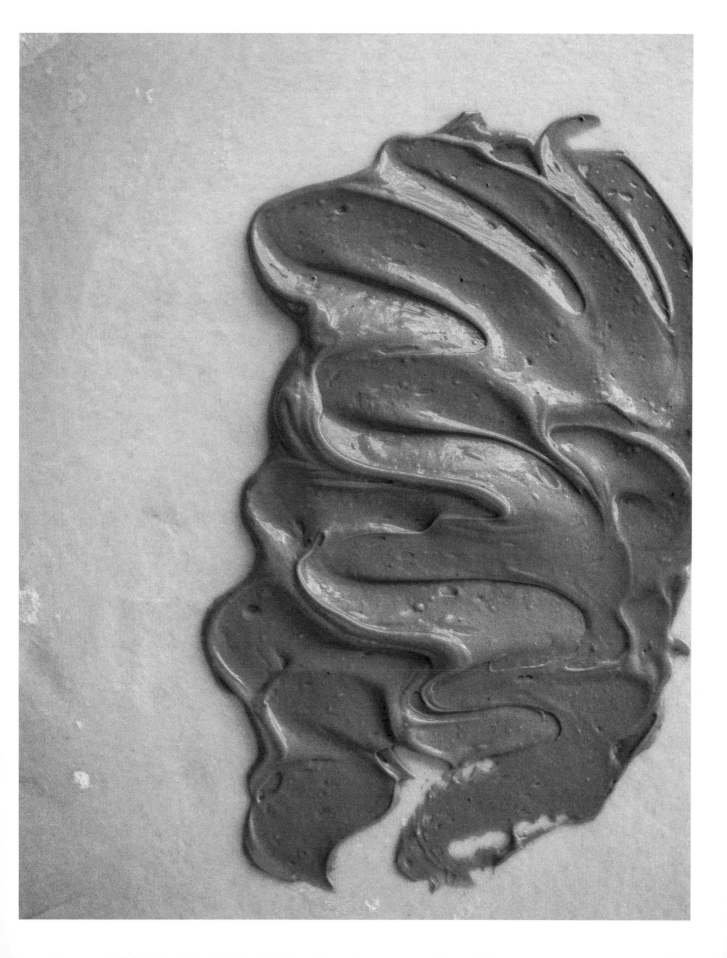

form and grassy, slightly creamy flavor also lend it wonderfully to all sorts of other applications. Both in Japan and, more and more frequently, here in the United States, you will find it in everything from chocolate to lattes to any kind of baked good imaginable. There are several grades of matcha, and for anything other than drinking it in traditional tea, you only need the most affordable grade. I prefer *Maeda-en* culinary-grade matcha powder, which you can find for a good price on Amazon.

RICE VINEGAR. Any recipe calling for rice vinegar, and not Chinkiang black vinegar, is referring to a sweet, delicate rice vinegar more commonly used in Korea and Japan. If you can't find rice vinegar, use another mild, mellow vinegar like white wine vinegar or apple cider vinegar.

SESAME OIL. Just as it sounds, sesame oil is oil pressed from sesame seeds. It is toasty, nutty, and deeply savory; because of its low smoke point, it is most often used as a flavor enhancer in Chinese, Japanese, and Korean cooking, rather than as an oil for cooking. I like *Kadoya* brand.

SESAME SEEDS. There are generally two types of sesame seeds, *black* and *white*. Black sesame seeds are unhulled, and have just a slightly deeper, more bitter taste than their white counterparts. I find that they're often a welcome complement in sweet desserts and treats for that reason, adding a toasty, smoky and nutty undertone. Where these recipes do not specify and call simply for toasted sesame seeds, however, either black or white sesame seeds will do.

SHAOXING RICE WINE. Shaoxing rice wine is wine fermented from sticky rice. It has a fragrant, distinctive flavor, and finds its way into all sorts of Chinese cooking, usually to mellow out and enhance the flavor of meat or seafood. Any brand

you find in a Chinese supermarket will likely do, but if you don't have access to one, you can easily use *dry sherry* or *sake* instead. Both have a slightly different flavor, but neither substitution will make a huge impact. However, avoid replacing Shaoxing with rice vinegars or mirin—rice vinegar is, well, vinegar, and thus has a very different taste, and although mirin *is* a rice wine, it is seasoned and often much sweeter.

SOY SAUCE. Made primarily from fermented soy beans, soy sauce is ubiquitous across the States, and is the most common way to add salty, savory flavors to Asian cooking. There are two types used in this book: light and dark. *Light soy sauce* is the one you find on the table at Asian restaurants and in almost any supermarket these days; it is the saltier, more flavor-forward soy sauce. *Kikkoman* brand light soy sauce is easily accessible and reliable. *Dark soy sauce*, by contrast, is less salty, but thicker, viscous, and deeply pigmented, with an almost molasses-like flavor. It is used to get the deep-red color found in many soy-braised dishes, as well as to add a slight tangy sweetness. Although traditionalists may disagree, the absence of dark soy sauce will not ruin your dish. If you can't find it, a touch of molasses with a touch more light soy sauce is a reasonable substitute—only the color of the dish will not be the same. *Lee Kum Kee* and *Pearl River Bridge* make good dark soy sauces.

Rice

In our household, it's not a complete meal without rice. We almost always use short- or medium-grain white rice, like *Kokuho Rose* or *Calrose*. Unless I'm making congee (page 24), I cook rice the "traditional" Asian way—that is to say, with a rice cooker. It is best rinsed several times before cooking, until the water begins to run clear.

Flours

FLOUR. There are a two types of wheat flour used in this book. The first is *all-purpose*, with which you are likely familiar. All-purpose flour is, as its name suggests, your friend in nearly everything, with a medium amount of protein that gives just enough springiness to a baked good without making it too dense. You will find it used here in cakes, soft breads like Steamed Buns (page 64), and sweet enriched breads like cinnamon rolls (page 241). I am forever a fan of *King Arthur Flour*, though for all-purpose flour any supermarket brand is likely to serve you just fine.

The second type of wheat flour used in this book is *bread flour*, which has a higher percentage of protein to help build more strength and gluten in your baked goods, making it perfect for—you guessed it—lofty, chewy bread. Here the difference between King Arthur Flour and lesser-quality bread flours is more noticeable, as King Arthur Flour has a slightly higher protein content than most bread flours that makes it perform beautifully in bread.

I have found, however, that the most important factor for flour is not what brand you choose but *how you measure it*. A digital or analog kitchen scale is always your best bet in guaranteeing that a recipe will turn out how you want it, but if you don't have one, the way I like to measure my flour is the *spoon-and-sweep method*: Fluff up the flour in your bag, and use a spoon to scoop it gently into your measuring cup. Use a flat edge, such as a butter knife or bench scraper, to level it off, then use as directed. In my experience, this is the most reliable way to measure flour that is closest to the weight measurements called for in most recipes.

SWEET RICE FLOUR (ALSO CALLED GLUTINOUS RICE FLOUR, STICKY RICE FLOUR, OR MOCHIKO FLOUR). Sweet rice flour, in a category separate from wheat flour, is a type of flour made from sticky (or glutinous) rice—the slightly translucent, pleasantly chewy rice you might find in a sweet mango dessert or wrapped tightly in a lotus leaf at dim sum. When ground into flour and cooked, it becomes soft and pliant, almost gooey, and it has a place on the table in almost any Asian cuisine, as *mochi* in Japan, *nian gao* in China, *dduk* in Korea, and more. I strongly recommend using an Asian brand if you can find it, though *Koda Farms* in California makes a very good sweet rice flour called *Mochiko Blue Star Brand*, which is available in small 16-ounce boxes for no more than $1 to $2 each. I would caution against using *Bob's Red Mill* brand, which—while likely fine for other uses—did not have the same results for me as Koda Farms or Asian brands when used in traditional Asian recipes.

Salts

Before I started cooking in earnest, I figured salt was salt and that's all there was to it. Not quite. There are finishing salts and cooking salts; flaky sea salts like *Maldon* are the former, best sprinkled on a dish just before serving for a little savory zing. Within cooking salts, there are different tastes and different densities, and therefore different levels of "saltiness." A teaspoon of *Morton Salt*, for instance, will make your food taste saltier than a teaspoon of *Diamond Crystal*. All the measurements in this book are based on Morton's, which is one of the most widely available brands in any part of the country, but to be safe, a good practice is to start with only half or three-quarters of the amount of salt called for in the recipe and then adjust to your preference. While you should not be afraid to season

with salt—it really is a flavor enhancer and makes everything taste better, when used correctly—it is much easier to make something more salty than less salty.

Sundries

I do not peel *ginger root* before cooking with it. I just give it a good scrub and grate, mince, or slice away; that said, if you feel so inclined, a spoon is a great way to scrape off the skin without losing too much of the flesh.

I use *salted butter* for the table and *unsalted* for most everything else. If all you have is salted, no worries! Just reduce slightly the amount of salt called for elsewhere in the recipe. Eggs are usually *large*. Milk is usually *whole*, but almost everything in this book can be made with the milk of your choice instead.

Equipment

CARBON STEEL WOKS. Woks, especially those made from carbon steel, are invaluable to Chinese cooking. They heat quickly and evenly, they withstand the high temperatures used for stir-frying, and their steel imparts a distinctive but subtle flavor into the dishes they hold. Their shape, too, makes them perfect for everything from stir-frying to steaming, deep-frying, and braising. My childhood is filled with memories of my mother at the helm of a screaming-hot wok, unfazed at the din from a pile of cold vegetables hitting the hot steel, her face disappearing behind a column of steam.

A carbon steel wok is ideal, although stainless steel or cast-iron woks will do the trick if that's all you have. Look for one with a long wooden handle on one side and a short looped handle on the other; a 14-inch wok is a good size to start with. Unless you have a burner specifically designed to hold a round-bottomed wok, look for a wok with a flat bottom. Avoid nonstick woks; a properly seasoned carbon steel wok will gradually become more and more nonstick as you cook with it.

CAST-IRON SKILLETS. The cast-iron skillet is to Southern cooking as the wok is to Chinese cooking; those are the two most beloved workhorses in my kitchen. In many ways they are opposites—a wok heats extremely quickly, whereas cast-iron heats slowly but retains its heat for far longer. It creates the best crispy edges of any pan I've used, perfect for golden-brown pancakes, crisp cornbread bottoms, and beautifully seared crusts on steak. It's the reason I've taken to using a cast-iron skillet instead of a wok for Potstickers (page 157)—they turn out with a perfectly crunchy bottom every time. As a plus, since cast-iron skillets are one single piece, handle and all, they are perfect for transferring to the oven after your dish has been initially seared or cooked on the stovetop. (You should take care when handling, though, because their handles can get very hot!) Like woks, cast-iron skillets also need some love and care to properly season them for use.

STURDY SCISSORS. I think a good pair of large, sturdy scissors might be one of the most underrated tools in the kitchen. My Korean mother-in-law uses them for everything from snipping chewy Korean noodles into shorter pieces to cutting meat, and they're good for slicing pizza, snipping a roll of dough into segments, "slicing" scallions into the pan when you're too lazy to get out a cutting board, deveining shrimp, the list goes on. I don't know what I used to do without them.

OTHER GOOD EQUIPMENT TO HAVE. I also love a good cast-iron *Dutch oven* for slow-braised meats and stews; a *bamboo steamer*, for making steamed buns and steamed vegetables, though a metal steamer insert for a pot works well, too; *silicone spatulas* for getting every bit of cake batter out of the bowl (ones by *GIR* are my favorite); a *spider skimmer* for rescuing foods from boiling water or oil when they're done, and for removing scum from simmering liquids; a *kitchen scale*, digital or analog; *fish spatulas*, for anything that needs a delicate hand to flip (not just fish); an *instant-read thermometer* for cooking meat and baking bread; a *Microplane grater* for finely grating ginger and garlic; a *mandoline* to make quick work of slicing vegetables or fruit (look for ones by *Benriner*); and a Y-shaped *vegetable peeler*, because I am terrible at peeling with a paring knife.

BREAKFAST

SIMPLE CONGEE

Serves 2 or 3

2 cups cooked short- or medium-grain white rice, or ⅔ cup uncooked

6 to 7 cups water or chicken stock (for a savory congee), or more as needed

A FEW IDEAS FOR TOPPINGS (OPTIONAL)

1 to 2 tablespoons sugar per bowl

Pork floss (rousong, pork sung, or pork fu)

1 to 2 teaspoons sesame oil per bowl

2 teaspoons soy sauce per bowl

Soft-boiled or poached eggs (any size)

Shredded chicken

Scallions, sliced

Salt and black pepper, to taste

There is no dish that I associate more with comfort food and childhood memories of nurturing warmth than congee. In my household we called it *xi fan*. My husband grew up with the Korean equivalent, *jook*. By either name it is essentially a gentle, soothing rice porridge, made by simmering rice in more water than seems necessary, for longer than seems prudent, until the rice grains nearly melt into one another. The resulting mixture is milky-white, almost creamy. It is delicious when prepared both sweet and savory. A bowlful with a sprinkling of sugar is reminiscent of rice pudding for break-fast, or you can add a hearty handful of shredded pork floss; add a little sesame oil and soy sauce, and you have the cure-all that my mother made whenever I was sick as a child. Some leftover chicken and a soft-poached egg will turn it into a hearty lunch. The possibilities are myriad—some sugges-tions are included here, but there are so many more for you to explore.

1 In a medium saucepan over high heat, combine the rice and water. (If you like a thick congee, you can start with 5 cups of water and add more later as needed.)

2 Bring to a boil, then reduce the heat to medium-low, or low enough to keep the congee at a gentle simmer. Cook, stirring every 10 minutes or so, until the rice grains burst open and the congee reaches your desired consistency—if using cooked rice, 20 to 25 minutes; if using uncooked rice, about 1 hour. For a thinner congee, add more water near the end; for a thicker consistency, continue to cook until it thickens to your lik-ing. It will continue to thicken as it cools.

3 Add toppings and seasonings of your choice. My favorites as a child were simple: a bit of sugar for a sweet oatmeal-like breakfast, or both sugar and pork floss for a sweet-and-savory combination. For a more elaborate meal, add sesame oil, soy sauce, a soft-boiled or poached egg, shredded chicken, and sliced scallions, and season with salt and pepper to taste. Serve immediately!

NOTES

This recipe is easily halved or doubled as needed, and leftovers will reheat just fine, though you may need to add a few tablespoons of water to loosen the congee the next day.

cooking in the land of peking ravioli

I ARRIVED IN CAMBRIDGE, MASSACHUSETTS, ON a brilliantly sunny day in August. There was no hint of the legendary Boston winters I'd heard about—the air was thick and hot, my brick-paved, leafy campus slow-moving and sleepy. It was my orientation for three years of law school, and I had no idea what to expect, from either my newly pursued profession or the city in which I would pursue it.

My classmates and I spent our days in steeply tiered, horseshoe-shaped classrooms, scribbling notes on lectures and crossing our fingers that we wouldn't be one of the few interrogated by our professors about the reading that day. The evenings were for burying our noses in thick crimson textbooks, staining our fingertips with highlighters, and reading case after case for the next day, when we'd do it all over again. Surrounded by the most accomplished people I'd ever met and about eight hundred miles from home, I was more nervous than I'd ever felt in a new place. Was I meant to be a lawyer? Was everyone here smarter than me? *Did I have enough warm clothing?*

The cure to any fleeting homesickness I'd had during college was simple. Call home, hop in the car, and, three hours later, walk through the door into a kitchen filled with the sounds and smells of my mother's cooking—the crash and hiss of a heap of cold green beans hitting a hot wok (page 188), spicy lamb shanks simmering until fall-apart tender (page 164), a pot of "Russian" soup (page 141) sending wisps of steam up to the ceiling. Here, though, a plane flight stood between my family and me, and even though it was barely two hours in the air, home felt a world away.

So I did the next best thing I could think of—I figured out how to bring my mother's food to Boston, instead.

The dorm kitchen was what you might politely call "economical," with a white microwave perched above the stove, laminate on the counters, and two windows that propped open to look out over the sidewalk. It turned out that, unlike in undergrad, the communal kitchens in graduate school were used every evening, heavily and often, and not only to make break-and-bake cookies every once in a blue moon. Here we jockeyed for shelf space and labeled our Tupperwares in bold Sharpie marker, and occasionally came into the kitchen to find angry notes tacked to the refrigerator's chest like a scarlet letter, addressed to WHOMEVER ATE MY PIE.

I began to cook on Sunday nights to prepare meals for the week ahead, a self-enforced break from poring over case law, time that I devoted instead to my mother's stir-fried Green Beans & Minced Pork (page 188) over rice; Tea Eggs (page 184) marinating in their dark, murky liquid; or sticky-sweet fillets of soy-glazed salmon (page 118). At first, I spent much of that time on the phone with my mother—*How much Shaoxing wine do I add? What does Shaoxing wine even look like? How many star anise?* I learned that the tiny flecks of fried goodness my mother added to her fried rice were Crispy Fried Shallots (page 126), and that I could make them myself; I peered at cubes of pork belly and wondered if the sauce was reducing the right way for Red-Cooked Pork (page 149). At the end of the night I lined up a tiny army of Tupperwares, filled them with my week's bounty, and stacked them neatly in the dorm refrigerator. (Thankfully, no one stole mine.)

With every week that passed, law school became more normal, and New England became more familiar. I bought a puffy, mystifyingly toasty down jacket and trudged to class in fleece-lined boots. I made friends with whom I shared tea eggs and course outlines. My one-hundred-square-foot single room went from cramped to cozy, filled with steam rising out of a tiny 1-cup rice cooker, a bowl of scrambled eggs with jammy tomatoes (page 195) on my desk. My newfound security, and my growing feeling that Cambridge could be home, wasn't completely due to food—but it helped, every step of the way.

All kinds of food can be comforting—the extra-long strings of melted cheese from a piping-hot pizza, a steaming bowl of ramen. The chewy sturdiness of "Peking ravioli," Boston's version of potstickers, swimming in chili oil and dark sauce. Making Chinese food the way my mother taught me, linking my childhood kitchen in South Carolina to my new one in Cambridge by the tenuous reception of a cell phone, was a special kind of comfort that has stayed with me, and that I encounter every time I break in a new kitchen in a new apartment or a new city. No matter how foreign or strange a place might be—it is home when filled with the food I love best.

SESAME-SOY SAVORY OATMEAL

Serves 1

It had never occurred to me that oatmeal could be savory until I came upon my mother-in-law one day, eating bites of oatmeal dolloped onto strips of toasted nori like tiny seaweed tacos. But then it made perfect sense. After all, congee is nothing more than oatmeal's rice-based cousin, and I'd grown up enjoying congee both sweet and savory. Why should oatmeal be any different? This savory oatmeal is my new go-to recipe when the fridge is empty and I'm looking for a satisfying pantry meal. The egg adds just a bit of welcome protein, which you can stir into the pot with the heat off, or if you have pasteurized eggs, just crack directly into the oatmeal right before you eat. The sesame seeds bring a little crunch and texture, and the sesame oil, soy sauce, and nori are, as in most applications, the ultimate way to create a deeply flavorful meal from practically nothing at all.

1 cup water

½ cup old-fashioned oats

1 large egg

1 to 2 teaspoons soy sauce

½ teaspoon sesame oil

1 teaspoon sugar (optional)

1 teaspoon toasted sesame seeds, or more to taste, for garnish

Shredded nori, for garnish

Bring the water to a boil in a small saucepan. Add the oats and simmer until cooked to your liking, about 5 minutes. Remove from the heat and quickly whisk in the egg until incorporated. Add the soy sauce, sesame oil, and sugar (if using), adjusting to taste as needed. Top with sesame seeds and shredded nori and serve hot.

NOTES

For a creamier oatmeal, add the oats to the saucepan while the water is cold.

OUR FAVORITE ENRICHED BREAD
(FOR HAM & EGG BAKED BUNS, CHAR SIU BUNS, BLACK SESAME–STUFFED FRENCH TOAST, PEANUT BUTTER & CONDENSED MILK TOAST)

Makes 1 tall 9 × 5-inch loaf or 12 to 16 buns

FOR THE DOUGH

½ cup whole milk

1½ teaspoons active dry yeast or instant yeast (see Notes)

2½ cups (about 320 grams) bread flour, plus up to ¼ cup (30 grams) more for kneading

2 tablespoons sugar

1 tablespoon nonfat dry milk powder (optional)

½ teaspoon salt

1 large egg

2 tablespoons unsalted butter, very soft

FOR THE TANGZHONG

6 tablespoons water

2 tablespoons (15 grams) bread flour

TO BAKE

1 egg (any size), mixed with a splash of water, for egg wash (optional)

Yeast bread is one of those things that intimidated me incredibly the first time I attempted it, but immediately hooked me for life after that. It's true what they say—kneading dough into a soft, supple cloud is therapeutic, and watching that cloud rise is nothing short of magical. Baking with yeast feels mercurial at first, but with a few fail-safes built in, like scalding the milk first and proofing the yeast before you use it, I find that it can be pretty comforting and predictable, after all.

This particular bread has its origins in a famed Hokkaido milk bread recipe by Christine Ho. Milk bread is a rich treat that incorporates heavy cream and milk powder for a lovely, slightly sweet bread, and Christine's wonderful recipe uses *tangzhong*, a kind of roux-like starter, to give the bread a lighter and fluffier texture. Because Christine's original recipe is in metric measurements and intended for a bread machine, I first tweaked it to be made with US measurements and by hand. Gradually, I fiddled with it just a tad more, lightening it a bit by replacing the cream with more milk and making the milk powder optional, for a slightly simpler, more everyday bread. The result is this recipe—a soft, airy bread that is enriched but not *too* rich, perfect for everything from decadently thick toast in An HK-Style Breakfast (page 37) to Char Siu Barbecue Pork Buns, Two Ways (page 71) to Ham & Egg Baked Buns (page 35). If you have any left a few days later, it makes the perfect vehicle for Black Sesame–Stuffed French Toast (page 43).

---

1 *The night before, or at least 2 hours before baking:* In a small saucepan over medium heat, bring the milk just to a boil, 2 to 3 minutes, or heat the milk to a boil in a small microwave-safe bowl in the microwave, about 1 minute. (This scalds the milk to kill any enzymes that might prevent the yeast from doing their thing.) Set aside to cool slightly. If you find a film on the surface of the milk after heating it, just pour the milk through a sieve.

(recipe continues)

2 *Next, make the tangzhong:* In a small saucepan, whisk together the water and bread flour until no lumps remain. Heat over medium-low, whisking constantly, until the mixture begins to resemble a roux-like gel, about 2 minutes. As soon as lines begin to appear in the mixture when stirred, remove from the heat and transfer to a small, clean bowl. Let cool to room temperature.

3 *Prepare the dough:* When the milk is just warm but no longer hot, about 100°F to 110°F, sprinkle the active dry yeast on top and let sit until foamy, 5 to 10 minutes. (See Notes if using instant yeast.) If the milk-yeast mixture does not foam, you may want to start over to make sure your yeast is active.

4 Meanwhile, in a large bowl, whisk together the flour, sugar, milk powder (if using), and salt. If not using a scale, take care to use the spoon-and-sweep method for measuring your flour (page 19), since too much flour can make the bread dense.

5 Once the yeast has foamed, add the tangzhong and the egg to the milk-yeast mixture, and whisk until well combined.

6 Make a well in the flour mixture and pour in the wet ingredients. Stir with a wooden spoon or silicone spatula until the mixture forms a loose, shaggy dough, then switch to using your hands. The dough should be sticky and soft but not gloppy, and should hold its form. Knead until the dough forms a semi-smooth ball, about 5 minutes. If it sticks too much as you knead, sprinkle flour over your hands and the dough as needed (I usually use 2 to 3 tablespoons).

7 Add the butter to the dough, 1 tablespoon at a time, kneading after each addition. Add the second tablespoon of butter only after the first has been evenly incorporated. The kneading will be slippery and messy at this point, but just keep kneading and it should eventually form a soft and pliable dough that's easy to work with. Knead until the dough becomes smooth and elastic, an additional 4 to 5 minutes.

8 Place the dough in a large bowl with plenty of room (no need to grease) and cover with plastic wrap or a damp dish towel. Let rise in the refrigerator overnight until well doubled, at least 8 hours. (Alternatively, you can let it rise at room temperature for 2 hours or so, until well doubled. I prefer a longer rise, to give the flavor time to develop and to split up the labor. The dough should be fine for up to 24 hours.)

9 *The next day, at least 1 hour before baking:* Shape the loaf as desired, then let rise a second time, this time until the dough bounces back very slowly when pressed with a fingertip, but an indent remains visible, about 1 hour.

10 *Just before the dough is done rising:* Preheat the oven to 350°F and line a tall 9 × 5-inch loaf pan (I like to use a Pullman pan) with parchment paper. Brush the dough with egg wash if desired, then bake, uncovered, for 30 to 40 minutes, until golden-brown on top and an instant-read thermometer inserted into the center reads 200°F. Enjoy!

NOTES

If using instant yeast, use the same amount as active dry yeast, but mix it in with the dry ingredients instead of adding it to the scalded milk. I have found SAF Instant Yeast (available at amazon.com) to be wonderful and reliable, yielding yeast goods that are fluffier, softer, and more flavorful than most.

To shape the bread in the "humped" shape typical of Hokkaido milk bread, divide the bread into 4 equal pieces. Roll each piece into a long oval. Fold the oval lengthwise into thirds, to form a long, skinny rectangle. Roll the rectangle up into a short, wide roll. Repeat with the remaining 3 pieces, then place the rolls into the pan, swirls facing out to the sides.

For a regular sandwich loaf–style bread, roll the dough out into an 8-inch square, or thereabouts. Roll the square up like you're making cinnamon rolls, then place it into the loaf pan with the seam down.

HAM & EGG BAKED BUNS

Makes 8 large buns

One of my favorite bakeries in Hong Kong was a small, open-air stall on the corner of a bustling street that presented rows of fluffy buns and soft rolls to passersby. The line there moved helter-skelter, with orders barked and delivered in seconds, and when they sold out for the day, they closed. The one I liked best—if I could get there in time to get it—was a Spam-and-egg baked bun, with the Spam peeking out demurely from inside pillowy milk bread. It reminded me of the ham-and-egg breakfast sandwiches emblematic of a certain fast-food chain here in the United States, but far more portable, with an airy, gently sweet dough jacket that leaves English muffins in the dust.

---

1 While the dough for the bread is rising, slice the ham into 8 pieces about 2 inches wide by 4 inches long. (If using Spam, it will already be this size when sliced.) If you have some odds and ends, that's fine; you can layer them together when the time comes.

2 In a 12-inch nonstick or cast-iron skillet, heat 1 tablespoon of oil over medium until shimmering. Add the meat and cook until lightly browned, 3 to 4 minutes. Flip and let the other side brown lightly, another 1 to 2 minutes, then remove from the pan and set aside.

3 Wipe out the skillet and return to low heat. In a large liquid measuring cup, whisk together the eggs, salt, and pepper until combined. The mixture should equal about 1½ cups beaten egg. Add another tablespoon of oil to the skillet and swirl until well-coated. When the oil is hot, after 2 to 3 minutes, add half the egg mixture (about ¾ cup) to the pan. Cook until the egg is nearly solid. Fold the bottom third of the egg onto the middle, then fold the top third down over the bottom third, letter-style. The egg should form a large 4 × 12-inch omelet. Remove the omelet from the pan and set aside. Repeat with the remaining oil and remaining egg mixture. Slice each omelet into 4 equal pieces, to create 8 pieces that are 4 inches long and a little over 2 inches wide. Both the egg and ham slices can keep in the refrigerator until the dough is finished rising.

(recipe continues)

1 batch Our Favorite Enriched Bread (page 30), prepared to the beginning of the first rise

12 ounces ham or Spam

3 tablespoons vegetable oil or other neutral oil, divided

6 large eggs

¼ teaspoon salt

⅛ teaspoon black pepper

All-purpose flour, for rolling

1 egg mixed with splash of water, for egg wash

4 When the bread dough is fully doubled, turn it out onto a well-floured surface and roll it into a 12-inch square. Cut in half to form 2 large 6 × 12-inch rectangles. Cut each of these strips widthwise into 4 pieces to form 8 smaller 3 × 6-inch rectangles.

5 Place a slice of ham and a slice of egg across the center of each strip to form a cross shape. Fold the edges of the dough around the ham and egg, letter-style. Pinch the seams together to seal and flip the bun seam-side down. Place onto a baking sheet and repeat with the remaining components. Layer any odds and ends of ham and egg together in a bun, if needed. Cover with a damp dish towel and let rise again until doubled, about 1 hour.

6 Meanwhile, preheat the oven to 350°F. Once the dough has doubled in size, brush the egg wash over the dough and bake for about 20 minutes, until golden-brown on top. Enjoy! Leftovers will keep in the freezer for several months, and can be reheated briefly in the microwave or wrapped in foil and heated in a 400°F oven for 10 to 15 minutes, until warmed through.

AN HK-STYLE BREAKFAST
(CONDENSED MILK TOAST & YUANYANG)

Serves 2

Several years ago, I was lucky enough to call Hong Kong my home for a few too-short months in my third year of law school. In that time I felt I barely scratched the surface of all the food the city had to offer—from its iconic mooncakes, enjoyed one rich sliver at a time, to bowls of rippling egg noodles hiding plump wontons in their midst and skewers of neon-yellow curry fish balls handed to me in a Styrofoam cup at a street stall, to towering mounds of steamed pork *yuk beng* at a small open-air restaurant, where a bare light-bulb, fixed to an overhang, cast a buttery circle of light over the three or four plastic tables in its purview.

Hong Kong's bustling tea restaurants, or *cha chaan teng,* were some of my favorite destinations for breakfast. In a way they are as fiercely unique as the city itself, offering an idiosyncratic blend of Western and Asian cuisine: quintessentially Hong Kong–Style Milk Tea (page 262) served alongside nostalgia-inducing Ovaltine; fish ball noodle soup alongside spaghetti. *Cha chaan teng* fare is food that seems impossibly good in light of its simplicity—silky, fluffy scrambled eggs on white bread with the crusts neatly sliced off, macaroni noodles and slivers of ham floating in a translucent broth, or extra-thick, sky-high slices of toast slathered with sweetened condensed milk, melted butter, and sugar, peanut butter, coconut jam, or a combination of all of the above. Happily, the last is so easy to create that you hardly need a recipe to make it in your own kitchen; slicing the bread nice and thick yields a toast that is crisp-edged but still creamy inside, and it can be topped with whatever you like. I find it is best enjoyed with a hot cup of *yuanyang,* Hong Kong's particular brand of part milk tea, part coffee morning caffeine.

2 thick-cut (1-inch) slices Our Favorite Enriched Bread (page 30), or your favorite soft white bread

¼ cup peanut butter, or to taste

2 to 4 tablespoons sweetened condensed milk

2 mugs Hong Kong Coffee Tea (Yuanyang) (page 265)

Toast the bread to your liking. Spread 2 tablespoons peanut butter (or more or less, as desired) on each slice, then drizzle generously with sweetened condensed milk. Enjoy with a hot mug of yuanyang.

KIMCHI-BRINED SPICY
CHICKEN BISCUITS

Makes 4 biscuit sandwiches

¼ cup kimchi liquid

1 tablespoon minced garlic
(2 to 3 cloves)

1 tablespoon gochugaru,
plus 1 to 2 teaspoons more
for dredging (optional)

1 teaspoon salt

½ teaspoon black pepper

1 pound boneless, skinless
chicken thighs (4 small
thighs)

1 batch My Favorite
Sunday Biscuits (page 53),
cut into 4 large 4-inch
rounds

1 large egg

½ cup (63 grams)
all-purpose flour

½ cup cornstarch

1 cup vegetable oil or
other neutral oil, or more
as needed for frying

Sliced cheese of your
choice (optional)

Back in the days when slowing metabolisms were a distant concern, spicy chicken biscuits were my to-go breakfast of choice on the way to school: crispy fried chicken thighs sandwiched between tender, cloud-like biscuits, and ideally draped with a melting slice of cheese, all wrapped up in crackly wax paper. More than a decade later, it's probably fortunate that I've moved out of the South and such things aren't nearly as accessible, but every once in awhile, a spicy chicken biscuit becomes my weekend project on a lazy morning. This version was born when I had a cup or so of kimchi brine left in a large tub of kimchi we'd just used up. Rather than toss the leftover brine, you can use it—along with some spices for extra kick—to tenderize and flavor chicken, just as a salt brine would. Breaded and fried the traditional way, then tucked into My Favorite Sunday Biscuits, this is a nostalgic, yet slightly transformed incarnation of my childhood favorite.

---

1 *The night before, or at least 1 to 2 hours before eating:* Whisk together the kimchi liquid, garlic, gochugaru, salt, and pepper. Place the chicken thighs in a gallon Ziploc bag or a shallow baking dish and pour the kimchi mixture over the chicken, making sure the mixture is evenly distributed. Marinate for 1 to 2 hours, ideally overnight, turning the chicken occasionally.

2 *The day of:* If you haven't already, make the biscuits. While they're baking, prepare the chicken. Remove the thighs from the marinade, collecting any marinade that drips off into the original container, and set aside. You should have about ¼ cup of marinade; pour it into a shallow bowl and add the egg. Whisk until combined. In a separate shallow bowl, whisk together the flour and cornstarch. If you'd like the chicken to be on the spicier side, add the extra gochugaru here. Dip each piece of chicken into the egg mixture, then dredge it thoroughly in the flour. Set aside to let the coating adhere.

(recipe continues)

3 Pour the oil into a cast-iron skillet or heavy-bottomed pot, aiming to fill it about ½- to ¾-inch deep. Heat the oil to between 350°F and 375°F. A deep-fry thermometer is especially handy for this, but if you don't have one, a wooden chopstick or spoon will bubble energetically when the oil hits this temperature. (While you're waiting for the oil to heat up, check on the biscuits if they're not yet done; remove from the oven and let cool while you fry.)

4 When the oil is fully hot, add half the chicken pieces, taking care not to crowd the pot, and let them bubble merrily until golden-brown underneath, 6 to 7 minutes. Flip and let the opposite side turn golden-brown as well, another 5 to 6 minutes. Remove and drain on paper towels. Repeat with the remaining half of the chicken.

5 Split open the biscuits and make a sandwich with the chicken pieces and a slice of cheese, if desired. Enjoy immediately.

BLACK SESAME–STUFFED FRENCH TOAST

Serves 2 to 4

French toast is a perennial favorite of mine when it comes to indulgent week-end breakfasts. I can never get enough of the play on textures between the custardy innards and the crisp, slightly chewy exterior, or the subtle savory-meets-sweet combination of egg and maple syrup. This particular version is inspired by the Chinese sweet dumpling soup dessert called *tangyuan*. My favorite *tangyuan* are the ones stuffed with a nutty black sesame filling that flows out, molten and inky, when you bite into a dumpling. It's possible that this filling works even better in French toast than in a sweet rice dumpling—the nutty, smoky sweetness and slightly sandy texture is a robust contrast against the eggy, custardy toast. Even as someone who loves French toast in any incarnation, I think it's one of the best versions I've ever had.

1 In a small, dry skillet, toast the black sesame seeds over medium heat until a few seeds jump in the pan and they start to smell toasty (but not burnt!), 2 to 3 minutes. In a food processor or blender, combine the sesame seeds and sugar and process until very fine and sandy, about 2 minutes. Reserve 2 tablespoons of the sesame-sugar mixture, then add the diced butter to the remaining mixture and blend again until a wet paste forms, 1 to 2 minutes.

2 In a large, shallow bowl, whisk together the eggs, vanilla (if using), and 1 tablespoon of the reserved sesame-sugar mixture until thoroughly combined. Add the milk and whisk again to blend. Cut each slice of bread nearly in half, leaving a "hinge" at the end. Drop generous dollops of the black sesame filling into the center of each slice and use the hinge to close the two halves of the slice around the filling.

3 In a large nonstick or cast-iron skillet, heat 1 tablespoon of butter or oil over medium until the butter has melted or the oil is shimmering. Place 2 slices of bread in the egg mixture until one side is soaked in egg, then flip and let the other side soak. Add both slices to the skillet and cook, swirling the pan occasionally, until browned on the bottom, about 3 minutes. Flip the slices and cook, swirling the pan occasionally, until the other side is browned, about 3 more minutes. Transfer to a plate and repeat with the remaining tablespoon of butter or oil and the remaining slices of bread. Serve with sweetened condensed milk and an extra sprinkling of black sesame sugar over top, and enjoy immediately.

FOR THE BLACK SESAME FILLING

½ cup plus 1 tablespoon black sesame seeds

½ cup plus 1 tablespoon sugar

½ cup (1 stick) unsalted butter, room temperature, diced

FOR THE FRENCH TOAST

2 large eggs

¼ teaspoon vanilla extract (optional)

⅔ cup whole milk

4 thick-cut (1-inch) slices day-old Our Favorite Enriched Bread (page 30), brioche, or challah

2 tablespoons unsalted butter or vegetable oil, for frying

Sweetened condensed milk, for serving

BUTTERMILK MOCHI PANCAKES

Serves 2

½ cup (63 grams) all-purpose flour

½ cup (70 grams) sweet rice flour, like Mochiko Blue Star

1 tablespoon sugar

1 teaspoon baking powder

½ teaspoon baking soda

¼ teaspoon salt

1 large egg, separated

½ cup Greek yogurt

½ cup milk of your choice

2 tablespoons unsalted butter, melted and cooled, plus more for the pan and for serving

Maple syrup, for serving

For years, the only pancakes I ever had were from a box mix. They were usually made by my father, who could flip them with just a flick of his wrist, and whose instructions on how to make pancake mix were simply to "add water until it looks right." As the first pancakes I ever had, these will always hold a special place in my heart. Still, in my own kitchen, I've transitioned slowly from box mix pancakes to pancakes made from scratch, which are hardly more difficult but wonderfully tender, fluffy, and flavorful.

These mochi pancakes are a slight riff on the recipe that has become my tried-and-true over the years. Interestingly, a bit of sweet rice flour mixed with all-purpose flour results in pancakes that aren't dense and chewy like pure mochi is. Instead, they're just the slightest bit softer and more tender, with a faint milkiness that I like.

---

1 In a medium bowl, whisk together the flours, sugar, baking powder, baking soda, and salt. Add the egg yolk, yogurt, milk, and melted butter, and stir until just incorporated. Stir in the egg white until just combined.

2 Heat a 10- or 12-inch cast-iron or nonstick skillet over medium until a drop of water sizzles when it hits the pan. Lightly grease the skillet with butter, then use a measuring cup to drop ¼ cup batter onto the pan. When the edges of the pancake look dry and bubbles begin to pop in the center, 2 to 3 minutes, flip and cook on the second side until lightly golden, 1 to 2 more minutes. Remove to a plate and repeat with the remaining batter. If desired, use an ovenproof plate and place the finished pancakes in the oven on its lowest heat setting to keep them warm while you cook the rest. Serve immediately, with butter and maple syrup.

NOTES

If you don't have sweet rice flour, just use 1 cup (125 grams) all-purpose flour, and you'll still have my very favorite pancakes.

SPICED KABOCHA MUFFINS

Makes 6 muffins

As a sweets-obsessed wife to a husband who, mystifyingly, does not like them at all, I'm always searching for good small-batch recipes that can satisfy my sugar cravings without leaving me racing myself to finish a mountain of baked goods before they go stale. These kabocha muffins (or regular pumpkin muffins, if you want to use pumpkin purée) are the perfect example of that. They tick off every box for everything I want in a muffin recipe: sweet, wonderfully moist from the squash, and warmly fall-spiced, yielding just enough muffins to accompany my coffee for the week. If you're making them for a crowd, just double or triple the recipe.

1 Preheat the oven to 350°F and line a 6-cup muffin tin with liners.

2 In a large bowl, whisk together the kabocha purée, sugars, egg, oil, yogurt, and vanilla (if using).

3 In a separate medium bowl, whisk together the flour, baking powder, baking soda, spices, and salt. Add the flour mixture to the kabocha mixture and fold together until just incorporated, taking care not to overmix.

4 Fill the liners three-quarters full (tulip liners are great for this, since you can fill them up a little higher without worrying about a mess). Bake for 20 to 25 minutes, until a toothpick inserted into the middle comes out clean and the tops spring back when touched.

NOTES

As written, this recipe makes moist, delicate muffins that are almost cake-like. I've found that increasing the flour to 1 cup (125 grams) yields muffins that are slightly denser and a bit less sweet, with a nice crisp, crackled top when they first come out of the oven. They are worth trying.

You can also swap out half the all-purpose flour for whole-wheat, white whole-wheat, or sprouted-wheat flour by weight.

½ cup kabocha squash or pumpkin purée

¼ cup granulated sugar

⅓ cup packed light brown sugar

1 large egg

3 tablespoons vegetable oil or other neutral oil

2 tablespoons full-fat Greek yogurt

½ teaspoon vanilla extract (optional)

¾ cup (93 grams) all-purpose flour (see Notes)

½ teaspoon baking powder

¼ teaspoon baking soda

2 teaspoons pumpkin pie spice, or 1 teaspoon cinnamon, ½ teaspoon ground ginger, ¼ teaspoon ground nutmeg, and ¼ teaspoon ground cloves

Pinch of salt

SPICY GOCHUJANG EGGS IN PURGATORY

Serves 4 to 6

1 to 2 tablespoons olive oil

2 cups diced onion (1 to 2 onions)

1 tablespoon minced garlic (2 to 3 cloves)

Salt and black pepper, to taste

¼ cup minced fresh parsley (or perilla leaves, if you can get them), plus more for serving

1 (28-ounce) can diced or crushed tomatoes

¼ cup grated Parmesan cheese, plus more for serving

2 to 3 tablespoons gochujang

1 to 2 teaspoons brown sugar, light or dark (optional)

1 to 2 cups torn spinach or kale leaves, or other leafy greens (optional)

4 to 6 large eggs (depending on how many people you're serving)

Toast, for serving

Before *shakshuka* rose to its current level of incredible popularity and (belatedly) made its way into my kitchen, tomatoes and eggs had never cozied up together on my plate except in my mother's homestyle Chinese Scrambled Eggs & Tomatoes (page 195). Thank goodness my horizons were expanded. Eggs become extraordinary when coddled in a spicy tomato sauce and baked until wobbly in the center but firm on the edges. Hearty, flavorful, and filling, yet simple and even rather light, it's the stuff that lazy brunch or even weeknight dinner dreams are made of. This version is based on "eggs in purgatory," an Italian cousin to *shakshuka*, but the heat in the tomato sauce comes from my favorite Korean condiment, *gochujang*. The sweet, smoky spice turns out to be an ideal match for bright tomato sauce, with a touch of fermented tang that blends seamlessly into the tartness of the tomatoes; you'd never guess it was there amid the parsley and Parmesan, except for the subtle, addictive depth of flavor that makes it the perfect unexpected addition.

1 In a 10-inch skillet, heat the oil over medium until shimmering. Add the onion and garlic, season with salt and pepper, and cook until the onion begins to soften, 2 to 3 minutes. Add the parsley and cook for about 2 more minutes, just until parsley begins to soften and turn bright green.

2 Add the tomatoes, Parmesan, gochujang, and brown sugar (if using), and give everything a good stir. Season with salt and pepper, then lower the heat to medium-low and simmer for about 15 minutes, stirring occasionally. Taste and adjust the seasonings if needed. Add the greens (if using) and cook until just barely wilted. Spinach and other more tender leafy greens will take only 30 seconds to 1 minute; kale and other tough leafy greens will take longer, 3 to 4 minutes.

3 Make small indentations in the sauce for the eggs, one for each egg, and crack them into the pan. Cover the pan and cook until the whites are set and the yolks are still soft, 5 to 7 minutes (or longer, if you like your eggs more firm). Meanwhile, toast your bread. Once the eggs are cooked to your liking, remove from the heat and enjoy warm, sprinkled with additional Parmesan and parsley, and served with toast for dipping.

CHEDDAR-SCALLION BISCUITS, PLUS A FEW VARIATIONS

Makes 6 to 8 small (3-inch) biscuits or 4 large (5-inch) biscuits

6 tablespoons (¾ stick) unsalted butter, nearly frozen

2 cups (250 grams) all-purpose flour, plus more for dusting

1 tablespoon baking powder

¼ teaspoon baking soda

1 teaspoon salt

¼ teaspoon garlic powder (optional)

1 cup (4 ounces) shredded cheddar cheese

⅓ cup thinly sliced scallions (about 3 scallions)

½ cup full-fat Greek yogurt

½ cup whole milk (or 1 cup buttermilk, omitting the Greek yogurt)

1 large egg mixed with a splash of water, for egg wash (optional)

I came late to homemade biscuits. They were so widely available where I grew up in South Carolina, and so unimpeachably good at my most-frequented restaurants, that I couldn't imagine my own kitchen could produce biscuits that were half as fluffy and buttery. I was happily wrong. Homemade biscuits are so attainable, and the results so lofty, tender, and perfect, that every Sunday brunch at home should feature them. All you need is a gentle hand and, as with Pie Crust (page 231), a good dose of cold for all your ingredients, and you're just 30 minutes away from melt-in-your-mouth, scarf-an-entire-batch-in-one-sitting biscuits.

---

1 Preheat the oven to 425°F. Let the butter thaw briefly if it's fully frozen, 5 to 10 minutes. In a large bowl, whisk together the flour, baking powder, baking soda, salt, and garlic powder (if using). Using the largest holes on a box grater, grate the butter into the flour mixture. Use your fingers to toss the butter into the flour until all the butter shreds are just coated. Add the cheese and scallions and toss again to combine.

2 In a small bowl or liquid measuring cup, whisk together the yogurt and milk. Add three-quarters of the yogurt-milk mixture to the flour-butter mixture, and use a wooden spoon or silicone spatula to stir gently until a dough just comes together. If needed, use the remaining yogurt-milk mixture to moisten any dry bits that won't adhere to the dough. The dough should hold together easily and should not be crumbly, but it also should not be wet and sticky.

3 Turn the dough out onto a well-floured surface. Using as light a touch as you can, gently pat the dough into a rectangle about ½-inch thick. Fold the bottom third of the dough up and then the top third of the dough down over the bottom third, as though you are folding a letter. Gently pat down the dough to about ½ inch again, then fold letter-style. Repeat the patting and folding process one final time, then pat the dough out to 1-inch thick (or thicker if you want really sky-high biscuits).

4 Using a floured biscuit cutter, cut rounds from the dough, taking care not to twist the cutter when you remove the rounds—this ensures the biscuits will rise as nice and tall as possible. Gather the dough scraps and gently pat them into a 1-inch mass, and cut again until you've used up all the dough.

5 Place the rounds, sides gently touching, in a cast-iron skillet or on a baking sheet. If desired, brush some egg wash over the biscuits for a more golden top. Bake for 13 to 15 minutes, until golden-brown on top.

A FEW VARIATIONS

Omit the cheddar cheese, garlic powder, and scallions, and you have **MY FAVORITE SUNDAY BISCUITS**. Use them for Kimchi-Brined Spicy Chicken Biscuits (page 40).

If you can track down White Lily self-rising flour, a traditionally Southern flour made from softer white winter wheat, use 2 cups White Lily self-rising flour, omit the baking powder and baking soda, and reduce the salt to ½ teaspoon, for lighter, fluffier, **SOUTHERN-STYLE BISCUITS**. (You may find that these biscuits need less moisture from the yogurt-milk mixture—start with ½ cup, and figure out from there how much you need to keep the mixture holding together.)

For **BLUEBERRY DROP BISCUITS**, decrease the salt to ½ teaspoon and omit the cheddar, scallions, and garlic powder. Add ⅓ cup sugar and 1 cup frozen blueberries in with the dry ingredients, then quickly mix in the wet ingredients. While everything is still cold, very gently mix just until a dough forms, taking care not to mash the blueberries. Skip the pat-and-fold steps, and drop balls of the dough onto the cast-iron skillet, or slice into squares. While the biscuits are baking, make a quick glaze to go on top: Whisk together 1 cup confectioners' sugar, 5 tablespoons heavy cream, and ½ teaspoon vanilla extract. Drizzle the finished biscuits with the glaze and serve warm.

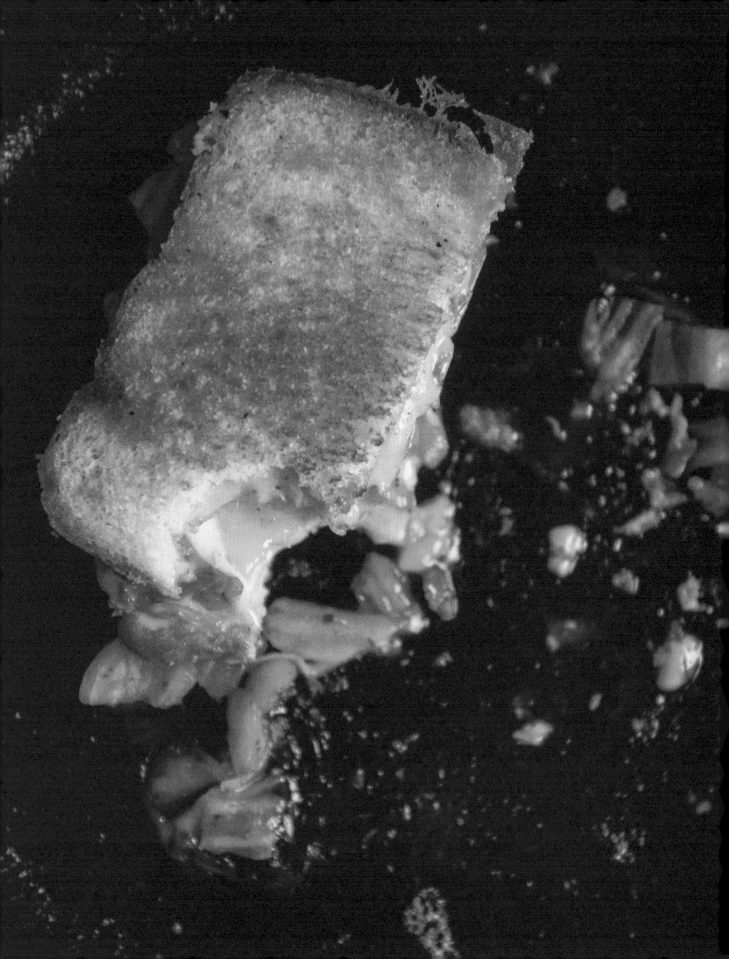

KIMCHI EGG & CHEESE

Makes 1 sandwich

The first time I made a kimchi grilled cheese, the reactions from my husband and my Korean mother-in-law were somewhere between perplexity and a kind of aggrieved horror. What did kimchi ever do to me, they felt, that it deserved to be mistreated with toasted bread and cheese? But I found the combination revelatory. Kimchi, with its fiery heat and pungent tang, adds a welcome brightness to the rich heft of grilled cheese, while the cheese and buttery toast, in turn, soften kimchi's piercing acidity. I was addicted. This version is a breakfast twist on that beloved sandwich, with a fried egg to add protein and a fun play on texture between the crisp egg white and the soft, golden egg yolk. With or without the egg, it is my very favorite way to ruin some perfectly good kimchi.

2 to 3 teaspoons vegetable or olive oil, divided

1 large egg

⅓ cup finely chopped kimchi, or more to taste

1 to 2 tablespoons salted butter (enough to thinly butter both sides of each slice), softened

2 (½-inch-thick) slices of your favorite bread

1½ ounces (2 slices) cheddar or American cheese

1 In a medium skillet, heat 1 to 2 teaspoons oil over medium until shimmering. Crack the egg into the pan and cook until the egg white is opaque but the yolk is still runny, 2 to 4 minutes. Carefully slide it onto a plate and give the skillet a quick wipe. Return the skillet to the heat and add another ½ teaspoon or so of oil. Roll it around to coat the pan, then add the kimchi and cook, stirring once or twice, until just hot and beginning to crisp around the edges, 2 to 3 minutes. Remove from the heat and set aside. Give the skillet another quick wipe or rinse.

2 Butter one side of each bread slice, taking care to spread the butter to the edges. Return the skillet to the stove over medium-low and heat until a drop of water sizzles on the pan. Add the bread slices and top each with a slice of cheese. Add the kimchi and the fried egg to one slice, then let the bread cook at a very gentle sizzle until golden-brown on the bottom, 3 to 4 minutes. If the bread isn't browning to your liking, increase the heat to medium. (I like to err on the side of lower heat, so that I don't risk burning it if I look away!)

3 Once the cheese is melted and the bottom of the bread is golden-brown, use a spatula to flip the cheese-only half onto the egg-and-kimchi half. Let cool briefly before serving.

LUNCH &
SMALL EATS

BLANK CANVAS CHINESE FRIED RICE

Serves 4 to 6

4 large eggs

Salt and white pepper

2 tablespoons shallot oil (from Crispy Fried Shallots, page 126) or vegetable oil, divided

1 tablespoon minced garlic (2 to 3 cloves)

1 cup diced onion (about 1 small onion)

6 ounces (about 1½ cups) diced ham or other cooked protein of your choice

1 cup frozen green peas, thawed

¼ cup sliced scallions (2 to 3 scallions)

1 to 2 cups vegetables of your choice (optional)

4 to 6 cups cooked white rice (see Notes)

1 to 2 tablespoons soy sauce (optional)

¼ cup Crispy Fried Shallots (page 126)

In my family, fried rice wasn't so much a recipe as a method, simply broad strokes of a meal to be colored in according to whatever you might have on hand that day. It always began with a few eggs and a generous pinch of salt, whisked vigorously with chopsticks and scrambled into small wisps in a screaming-hot wok. But it could go all sorts of ways after that—a generous handful of frozen peas, a finely diced onion, or maybe a few carrots; chopped honey ham, shrimp, crab, or diced *char siu* pork. Whatever we had, it went in, and the end result was a wok heaping with savory, hearty rice, to be kept warm on the stove over low heat, crackling softly and forming a delightfully crisp bottom crust, while everyone went back for seconds, thirds, and fourths.

I consider this recipe a "blank canvas" starting point for our family's fried rice. We love it as written, but it works just as well with an extra cup of diced carrots, a few sliced scallions, or some Chinese wood ear mushrooms in addition to the green peas and onions below; for your meat, you can try Char Siu Pork (page 76), shrimp, lump crabmeat, or *lap cheong* (Chinese sausage) in place of the diced ham, or throw in a combination of all of the above. The world is your fried-rice oyster.

---

1 Beat the eggs with ¼ teaspoon salt and a generous pinch of white pepper. In a large wok or skillet, heat a tablespoon of oil over medium-high until shimmering. Add the eggs and scramble to your liking; I find that breaking the eggs into smaller pieces makes for more flavorful fried rice. Remove from the wok and set aside.

2 Wipe out the wok and heat the remaining tablespoon of oil over medium-high until shimmering. Add the garlic and onion. Season generously with salt and white pepper and cook until the onions just begin to soften, 2 to 3 minutes. Add the ham and cook for another 1 to 2 minutes. Finally, add the green peas, scallions, other vegetables (if using), and the scrambled eggs, and stir until combined.

(recipe continues)

3 Add the rice and vigorously break up any lumps, stirring until everything is evenly distributed. Season with more salt and pepper, if needed, as well as soy sauce, if desired. Reduce the heat to its lowest setting and let sit for about 5 minutes, without stirring, to allow the bottom of the rice to crisp up. Top liberally with Crispy Fried Shallots, and enjoy! Leftovers will keep in the refrigerator for up to 1 week.

NOTES

There is a school of thought that, in order to avoid soggy fried rice, you must use day-old or days-old rice, chilled in the refrigerator until needed. I haven't always discovered this to be the case, and tend to find old, chilled rice somewhat difficult to break up in the pan. (On top of this, I hardly ever find myself in the happy circumstance of having enough leftover rice when a craving for fried rice hits!) As such, I prefer to simply make my rice with a little less water than usual in order to yield a slightly drier rice that breaks apart easily in the pan, allowing the individual grains to incorporate more evenly and flavorfully and absorb any moisture from the other mix-ins, to end up perfectly fluffy and delicious.

STEAMED BUNS
(FOR SCALLION BUNS, CHAR SIU BUNS, OR EGG CUSTARD BUNS)

Makes 12 to 16 buns

1 cup milk of your choice
(I use whole)

1 tablespoon oil

2 teaspoons active dry
yeast or instant yeast
(see Notes)

3 cups (375 grams)
all-purpose flour, plus
more for kneading and
rolling

¼ cup sugar

1 tablespoon nonfat dry
milk powder (optional)

½ teaspoon salt

When steamed instead of baked, bread becomes soft, white, and pillowy, with a cheerful bounce and a light yet satisfying chew. It's the kind of bread that forms the mainstay of Chinese breakfasts and comforting snacks, and I grew up sinking my teeth into steamed buns of all kinds. This basic dough is gently tweaked from my mother's recipe—it yields a creamy, gently sweet, springy-textured bread, ready to be twisted into steamed scallion buns, wrapped into pork buns, or filled with egg custard, or simply enjoyed all on its own with a glass of warm soy milk.

---

1 *The night before, or at least 2 hours before baking:* In a small saucepan over medium heat, bring the milk just to a boil, 2 to 3 minutes, or heat the milk to a boil in a small microwave-safe bowl in the microwave, about 1 minute. (This scalds the milk to kill any enzymes that might prevent the yeast from doing their thing.) Set aside to cool slightly until warm to the touch but not hot, about 100°F to 110°F. If you find a film on the surface of the milk after heating it, just pour the milk through a sieve. Stir in the oil, then sprinkle the yeast on top and let sit until foamy, 5 to 10 minutes. If the milk-yeast mixture does not foam, you may want to start over to make sure your yeast is active. (See Notes if using instant yeast.)

2 Meanwhile, in a large bowl, whisk together the flour, sugar, milk powder (if using), and salt. If not using a scale, take care to use the spoon-and-sweep method for measuring your flour (see page 19), since too much flour can make the dough dense. When the yeast is foamy, add the yeast mixture to the flour mixture and stir with a wooden spoon or silicone spatula until a dough forms.

3 Turn the dough out onto a floured surface and knead until smooth and elastic, 6 to 8 minutes. Place the dough in a large bowl with plenty of room (no need to grease) and cover with plastic wrap or a damp dish towel. Let rise in the refrigerator overnight, at least 8 hours. (Alternatively, you can let it rise at room temperature for 2 hours or so, until well doubled. I prefer a longer rise, to give the flavor time to develop and to split up the labor. The dough should be fine for up to 24 hours.)

4 *The next day, at least 1 hour before baking:* Once it's done rising, turn the dough out onto a floured surface and knead once or twice to deflate. At this point, you can shape the dough as desired for Egg Custard Steamed Buns (page 225), Char Siu Barbecue Pork Buns, Two Ways (page 71), or Steamed Scallion Buns (page 68).

5 If making plain buns (mantou), roll the dough into an 8 × 10-inch rectangle and then tightly roll that into a large cylinder. Cut the log into small 1- to 1½-inch-wide pieces, and cut out the same number of 4-inch parchment squares. Place each bun on a parchment square and let rise until the dough bounces back very slowly when pressed with a fingertip, but an indent remains visible, about 1 hour.

6 While the dough is rising, set up your steamer. If using a pot with a steamer basket, fill the pot with about 2 quarts of water and bring it to a boil over high heat. If using a bamboo steamer, fill a large wok or skillet with about 2 inches of water and bring to a boil over high heat. The water should be high enough that the rim of the bamboo steamer rests in the water, but not so high that the bottom of the basket touches the water.

7 Place 3 or 4 buns in each steamer tier, or however many will fit with a generous 2 to 3 inches between each bun. Reduce the heat to medium-low, or low enough to keep the water just at a gentle simmer, cover the steamer, and set it over the water. Let the buns steam until resilient when touched and cooked through, about 15 minutes. (You may want to place the remaining buns in the refrigerator to slow the rising while you steam the first batches.)

NOTES

To use instant yeast, use the same amount as active dry yeast, but mix it in with the dry ingredients instead of adding it to the scalded milk. I have found SAF Instant Yeast (available at amazon.com) to be wonderful and reliable, yielding yeast goods that are fluffier, softer, and more flavorful than most.

Variations on steamed bun recipes sometimes call for part cake flour for a lighter, fluffier texture, or baking powder or baking soda for more lift. In trying out each of these methods, I did not find an appreciable difference in the texture, but rather that they tended to create a dimpled surface on the bun, so I've kept things simple here.

STEAMED SCALLION BUNS
(XIANG CONG HUA JUAN)

Makes 12 to 16 buns

1 cup finely sliced scallions (8 to 9 scallions)

3 to 4 tablespoons vegetable oil or other neutral oil, or more as needed to moisten scallions

¼ teaspoon salt, plus more for sprinkling on top (optional)

1 batch Steamed Buns (page 64), prepared to the end of the first rise

All-purpose flour, for kneading and rolling

There are two things I find marvelous about these scallion buns. First, they're an ode to the power of the humble scallion, which so wholly infuses these rolls with a pungent, savory fragrance it's hard to believe that they, along with a bit of oil and salt, are the only thing separating these rolls from plain steamed *mantou*. And second, these rolls are practically license to play with your food. With just a few cuts and folds, they become the intricately twisted "flowers" that inspire their name in Mandarin: *hua* ("flower") + *juan* ("twist" or "curl" or "roll"). There are two techniques you can use, both of which are far easier than they sound on paper, but if they don't turn out how you imagine, never fear—the differences will only give them character, and after all, they all taste the same in the end.

1 In a small bowl, whisk together the scallions, vegetable oil, and salt. Cut out twelve to sixteen 6-inch squares of parchment paper to place underneath each bun.

2 When the dough has doubled in size, turn it out onto a floured surface and deflate. Divide the dough into 12 to 16 pieces. A dozen rolls will be quite large, about 6 inches across; more rolls will be, of course, smaller.

3 For each piece of dough, roll it out to an oval about 4-inches wide and 6-inches long (it doesn't have to be exact). Slice ribbons lengthwise into the oval, leaving about ½ inch at the top of the oval intact. Brush about 1 tablespoon of the scallion mixture across the dough, then pick up each end of the ribboned oval and twist the dough into a rope, with the ribbons forming a spiral. Either coil or knot the rope into a circle, and place it onto a square of parchment paper. Repeat with the remaining dough. (See Notes for alternative shaping methods.) When all the dough has been shaped into rolls, cover lightly with a damp dish towel or paper towels and let rest until the first batch of rolls you shaped has risen for 30 to 40 minutes, until the dough bounces back very slowly when pressed with a fingertip, but an indent remains visible.

(recipe continues)

4 While the dough is rising, set up your steamer. If using a pot with a steamer basket, fill the pot with about 2 quarts of water and bring it to a boil over high heat. If using a bamboo steamer, fill a large wok or skillet with about 2 inches of water and bring to a boil over high heat. The water should be high enough that the rim of the bamboo steamer rests in the water, but not so high that the bottom of the basket touches the water.

5 Starting with the buns you shaped first, place 3 or 4 in each steamer tier, or however many will fit with a generous 2 to 3 inches between each bun. Reduce the heat to medium-low, or low enough to keep the water just at a gentle simmer, cover your steamer, and set it over the water. Let the buns steam until resilient when touched and cooked through, about 15 minutes. (You may want to place the remaining buns in the refrigerator to slow the rising while you steam the first batches.)

6 Repeat with the remaining buns. Enjoy warm, sprinkled with salt, if desired. Leftovers can be frozen and reheated in the steamer or the microwave.

NOTES

For a simpler technique, you can shape the dough as though you are making plain Steamed Buns (page 64) or My Favorite Cinnamon Rolls (page 241). Roll out the dough into a large 12 × 14-inch rectangle, then spread the scallion mixture evenly across the dough, leaving a ½-inch border around the edges. Starting at a short end, roll the rectangle snugly into a log, then slice the log into about a dozen pieces. Steam as is, or press a chopstick down lengthwise on top of each piece, causing the roll to "fold" in the center and the swirls on either side of the bun to face upward, then tuck the ends underneath.

CHAR SIU BARBECUE PORK BUNS, TWO WAYS

Makes 12 to 16 buns, baked or steamed

In law school, I used to take a bus from Boston to New York that let off on the corner of Thirty-Fourth Street and Eighth Avenue in Manhattan. Just near there, squeezed between a Wendy's and a Burger King, was a tiny Chinese bakery that sold some of the tastiest barbecue pork buns I've ever had in New York. The steamed versions were fluffy and snow-white, with appealingly cracked tops; the baked ones were burnished golden yet soft and feathery inside. Both held mounds of deliciously sweet-yet-savory chopped pork in their bellies, which stained the dough a vibrant crimson when you bit into them. I could never choose between the steamed and baked varieties, and for a time, every return trip from New York found me clutching at least one of each, tucked neatly in their wax paper jackets, for the ride back.

Later, after I met my husband and visited his home in Hawaii for the first time, his family would introduce me to *manapua,* Hawaii's version of *char siu* buns. I had thought that my beloved pork buns could not be improved upon, but I was wrong. It turns out, all you have to do is make them bigger. *Manapua* were just like the *char siu* buns I knew, but impressively rotund and even squashier from all their extra heft. As I grew up eating *char siu* buns on pilgrimages to dim sum restaurants in neighboring Atlanta, my husband's family had been eating the same thing (only bigger), picked up after mass on Sundays from a tiny Chinese bakery in Mānoa.

Loving those pork buns as much as we both did, it was only a matter of time before I tried my hand at them in my own kitchen. I like to make both the steamed and the baked varieties; the wonderful thing about making them yourself is that you never have to choose. They're a labor of love, to be certain, but worth it for every soft, pork-filled pillow that emerges from the oven or steamer. As a bonus, any leftovers freeze wonderfully: To reheat, just wrap one in a damp paper towel and microwave for 30 seconds to 1 minute, or wrap it in foil and heat in a 350°F oven for 5 to 10 minutes, until heated through.

(recipe continues)

BAKED

1 *The night before, or at least 2 hours in advance:* Prepare Our Favorite Enriched Bread up to the start of the first rise.

2 *While the dough is rising, make the filling:* In a large skillet, heat a little vegetable oil over medium until shimmering. Add the pork, hoisin sauce, brown sugar, rice wine, soy sauce, oyster sauce, and white pepper and cook, stirring occasionally, until the sauce begins to thicken and turn viscous, 3 to 4 minutes.

3 In a small bowl, whisk together the cornstarch and water until smooth. Add the cornstarch slurry to the pan and continue to cook until the pork mixture can be mounded, another 1 to 2 minutes. Remove from the heat and refrigerate until ready to use.

4 *The day of:* Line two baking sheets with parchment paper or Silpat mats. When the dough has doubled in size, turn it out onto a floured surface and divide into 12 pieces for large buns (about 5 inches in diameter each), or 16 for medium (3 to 4 inches in diameter each). Roll each dough piece out to a 4- to 5-inch circle. Place 2 to 3 teaspoons of filling in the center of the circle, then fold the dough around the filling and pinch the edges together to seal them shut. Transfer to the lined baking sheet and repeat with the remaining dough pieces, leaving about 2 to 3 inches between each bun on the pan.

5 When all the buns are formed, cover with a damp dish towel and let rise for another hour or so, until the buns are puffy and doubled in size, and the dough bounces back very slowly when pressed with a fingertip, but an indent remains visible.

6 Meanwhile, preheat the oven to 350°F. Once the buns have finished the second rise, brush the egg wash generously over each one. Bake for 18 to 20 minutes, until golden on top. Enjoy warm.

NOTES

You can halve the filling if you prefer, freeze any you have left for your next bun-making party—or simply enjoy it with congee (page 24) or over rice.

(recipe continues)

FOR THE DOUGH

1 batch Our Favorite Enriched Bread (page 30), prepared to the start of the first rise

FOR THE CHAR SIU PORK FILLING

2 teaspoons vegetable oil or other neutral oil, or as needed

1½ pounds Char Siu Pork (page 76), diced small

¼ cup hoisin sauce

¼ cup packed dark brown sugar, or more to taste

¼ cup Shaoxing rice wine, dry sherry, or sake

2 tablespoons soy sauce, or more to taste

1 tablespoon oyster sauce

¼ teaspoon white pepper

2 tablespoons cornstarch

2 tablespoons water

TO BAKE

All-purpose flour, for rolling

1 large egg mixed with a splash of water, for egg wash

STEAMED

FOR THE DOUGH

1 batch Steamed Buns (page 64), prepared to the end of the first rise

FOR THE FILLING

1 batch Char Siu Pork Filling (page 73)

1 When the dough has risen, deflate the dough and knead it a few times. Divide the dough into 12 to 16 equal pieces and cut out the same number of 4-inch parchment-paper squares. Roll each piece of dough out into a 4- or 5-inch circle, aiming to roll the edges thinner than the center. Place 2 to 3 teaspoons of filling in the center of the circle and pinch the edges of the dough up around the filling to seal. Take care not to get the filling on the edges of the dough, which can keep them from sealing properly. (See opposite, though it doesn't need to be perfect if you steam the bun seam-side down.) Place the shaped bun seam-side down on a parchment square. Repeat until the remaining filling and dough is gone.

2 While the dough is rising, set up your steamer. If using a pot with a steamer basket, fill the large pot with about 2 quarts of water and bring it to a boil over high heat. If using a bamboo steamer, fill a large wok or skillet with about 2 inches of water and bring to a boil over high heat. The water should be high enough that the bamboo steamer rim rests in the water, but not so high that the bottom of the basket touches the water.

3 Starting with the buns you shaped first, place 3 or 4 in each steamer tier, or however many will fit with a generous 2 to 3 inches between each bun. Reduce the heat to medium-low, or low enough to keep the water just at a gentle simmer, cover the steamer, and set it over the water. Let the buns steam until the buns are resilient when touched and cooked through, about 15 minutes. (You may want to place the remaining buns in the refrigerator to slow the rising while you steam the first batches.)

4 Repeat with the remaining buns. Enjoy warm. Leftovers can be frozen and reheated in the steamer or the microwave.

NOTES

If you like, you can steam these with the pleats facing upward, which will make them more similar to the buns you might get at a dim sum restaurant. They won't look exactly like the craggy, cracked "smiling" *char siu* buns, but they may split open a bit as they steam. I prefer them seam-side down, *manapua*-style, for a neater appearance and more fully sealed bun.

CHAR SIU PORK

Serves 4 to 6

¼ cup hoisin sauce

¼ cup soy sauce

¼ cup honey

¼ cup packed dark brown sugar

2 tablespoons Shaoxing rice wine, dry sherry, or sake

2 teaspoons sesame oil

2 teaspoons oyster sauce (optional)

1 tablespoon minced garlic (2 to 3 cloves)

½ teaspoon Chinese five-spice powder (see Notes)

¼ teaspoon white pepper

2 pounds pork shoulder, sliced into 2-inch-thick strips

My love of glossy-red *char siu* barbecue pork goes back a long way. For a few months in my childhood, I lived with my grandparents in Changzhou, a town two hours east of Shanghai. It was there that I first remember enjoying *char siu* pork, and it took no time at all before my grandmother realized that my favorite treat was looking in my rice bowl and finding a neat row of crimson, tender roast pork slices, glistening with a sweet glaze and ready to be devoured with rice and bok choy.

Char siu or *cha shao* literally means "fork-roasted," and traditional *char siu* pork is roasted in large slabs to be hung tantalizingly in restaurant storefronts, beckoning to passersby. Luckily for us, slicing pork shoulder into thick strips and roasting it in a regular old oven will yield juicy, flavorful meat that's every bit as addictive. Enjoy it on its own over rice, then dice the leftovers and use in fried rice (see page 60) or fluffy pork buns (see page 71).

---

1 *1 day ahead, or up to 2 hours in advance:* In a medium bowl or liquid measuring cup, mix together all the ingredients except the pork shoulder. Place the pork shoulder in a large, shallow baking dish or a gallon Ziploc bag. Pour the marinade over the pork and let marinate for several hours, ideally overnight or up to 1 day in advance.

2 *When ready to cook:* Preheat the oven to 275°F. Place the pork slices on a baking sheet, reserving the marinade for basting. Bake for about 1 hour, brushing the marinade generously over the pork every 10 minutes, until the pork reaches an internal temperature of 160°F. If the pork is not yet tender to your liking, cover with foil and continue to bake for an additional 30 minutes, until a fork slides through the meat with less resistance. Let cool briefly, then slice and enjoy.

NOTES

Typically, *char siu* pork gets its deep red color from things like red fermented tofu or red yeast rice, and its lacquer-like shine from maltose syrup; these aren't terribly easy to come by in the United States, however, and I have found that my go-to recipe—while not as brightly vermilion as the pork you might find in a restaurant—does not suffer in the least without them.

To make your own Chinese five-spice powder, in a medium saucepan over medium, toast 2 star anise, 2 teaspoons Sichuan or regular peppercorns, 1 teaspoon whole cloves, 1 teaspoon fennel seeds, 1 teaspoon coriander seed, and 1 cinnamon stick until fragrant, 2 to 3 minutes. Place in a spice grinder or clean coffee grinder and grind to a fine powder.

DUMPLING DOUGH
(FOR POTSTICKERS, KIMCHI SUJEBI, GINGER-SCALLION CHICKEN & DUMPLINGS)

Makes 18 to 24 dumpling wrappers

2 cups (250 grams) all-purpose flour, plus up to ¼ cup (30 grams) more for kneading and rolling

½ teaspoon salt

¾ cup boiling water

It may seem like quite the endeavor to make your own dumpling wrappers, but in truth they couldn't be easier. There's something magical about the fact that it takes nothing more than flour, water, and a touch of salt to make something that's not just edible, but delicious—a pliable and toothsome vehicle for all kinds of fillings. And these hardy little wrappers show up in all sorts of other incarnations. As it turns out, the very same recipe for Chinese dumpling wrappers will make the hand-torn noodles in Korean *sujebi* (page 82), which in turn bears an uncanny resemblance to the "flat dumpling" in Southern chicken and dumplings (page 79). You can even swap out some of the all-purpose flour for semolina flour, use warm water instead of boiling, and, voilà, have yourself handmade orecchiette pasta. It's truly a jack-of-all-trades.

---

1 In a medium bowl, whisk together the flour and salt. Let the boiling water rest for a few seconds, then trickle it slowly into the flour while stirring with chopsticks or a silicone spatula. A wet dish towel placed under the bowl can help keep it in place while you stir.

2 After you've added all the water, continue to stir until the mixture becomes pebbly and shaggy, and the water is evenly incorporated. Make sure the dough is a comfortable temperature to touch, then use your hands to knead until the dough comes together into one mass. Turn it out onto a lightly floured surface and knead until smooth and taut, about 5 to 10 minutes. The dough should be fairly firm, not tacky, and should not stick to your hands or the bowl. If it is overly sticky, add a few more tablespoons of flour as you knead. Place in an airtight container or Ziploc bag and allow the dough to rest at room temperature for at least 15 minutes or up to 2 hours, or in the refrigerator for 1 day. In a closed container, the moisture will evenly distribute, allowing the dough to relax to a consistency that's easy to work with and roll out.

3 At this point, it's ready to be rolled out into wrappers for Potstickers (page 157) or torn into pieces for kimchi sujebi (page 82). You can also pop them into Ginger-Scallion Chicken & Dumplings (page 79), though those dumplings benefit from a bit of chicken stock in place of the boiling water.

GINGER-SCALLION CHICKEN & DUMPLINGS

Serves 4

For me, two kinds of dumplings come to mind when it comes to Southern cooking: the large, round variety akin to matzo balls that crop up both in chicken and dumplings and in desserts like blueberry dumplings; and the "flat dumplings" (or "slicks," depending on where in the South you call home). The latter is the sort I've always preferred with my chicken. You'll find all sorts of recipes for flat dumplings, some involving baking powder and others unleavened, some involving a few tablespoons of butter, but I was delighted to realize that their simplest incarnation was almost identical to something I'd been making all along—the dough for potsticker dumpling wrappers (page 78). So, of course, there was no question what recipe I'd be using in my own kitchen.

These chicken and dumplings get another slight Asian twist from a different kind of "southern" cuisine—Hainanese chicken and rice, a beloved staple from southern China. While the ingredient list might seem woefully short, simmering chicken with nothing more than a generous pile of sliced ginger and scallions results in a spicy, savory, and unexpectedly complex meal that is simple to prepare but deeply flavorful. You can add a drizzle of soy sauce or a dollop of chili garlic paste, if you'd like, but I've always found that this six-ingredient dish is all I need.

2 pounds chicken drumsticks or thighs, skin-on and bone-in

1½ teaspoons salt

3 or 4 scallions, sliced into 1-inch pieces (about ½ cup)

3 inches ginger root, sliced into ⅛-inch pieces (about ⅓ cup)

6 cups water

1 cup (125 grams) all-purpose flour, plus more as needed

OPTIONAL

Soy sauce, for serving

Chili garlic paste, for serving

---

1 *Make the soup:* Season the chicken generously with 1 teaspoon salt. Place it in a medium pot with the scallions, ginger, and water. (If desired, tie the ginger in cheesecloth to make it easier to remove later.) Bring to a boil over high heat, then reduce to medium-low, keeping the soup at a bare simmer.

2 *Make the dumpling dough:* After the soup has been simmering for about 30 minutes, start the dumplings. In a medium bowl, whisk together the flour and remaining ½ teaspoon salt. Ladle about 6 tablespoons broth and trickle it into the bowl of flour while stirring the flour with chopsticks or a silicone spatula. A wet dish towel under the bowl may help keep it in place while you stir. After you've added all the broth, continue to stir until the flour mixture becomes pebbly and the water is evenly incorporated. Make sure the dough is a comfortable temperature to

(recipe continues)

touch, then use your hands to knead the dough until smooth and taut, 5 to 10 minutes. The dough should be fairly firm, not tacky, and should not stick to your hands or the bowl. If it does, add more flour, a tablespoon at a time, until the dough is firm. Place in an airtight container or a Ziploc bag and allow to rest while the broth simmers for another 25 to 30 minutes (for a total of 1 hour altogether).

3 Skim any scum off the top of the broth and remove the ginger, if you'd like. Transfer the chicken to a plate or cutting board and use a fork to pull the meat from the bones. Return the meat to the pot and let the soup continue to simmer gently while you make the dumplings.

4 *Form the dumplings:* By now, the dumpling dough should be nice and pliable after its rest. The traditional method of preparing flat dumplings is to roll the dough out to a large rectangle, ¼ inch or less in thickness, and then slice the rectangle into 1 × 2-inch strips. Alternatively, you can form them the way noodles are torn for kimchi sujebi (page 82): Pinch off a tablespoon of dough and pull it in half so that it forms 2 flat pieces. Flatten the pieces to about ¼ inch or less, if needed, but otherwise the pieces need not be uniform. Roughly torn edges create a nice texture. Repeat until the dough is gone.

5 Bring the soup back to a lively simmer over medium heat, then drop the dumpling pieces into the pot. Simmer until the dumplings float to the surface, 1 to 2 more minutes, then serve, with soy sauce and chili garlic paste on the side, if desired.

SPICY KIMCHI HAND-TORN NOODLE SOUP
(KIMCHI SUJEBI)

Serves 2 or 3

½ batch Dumpling Dough (page 78), prepared to the resting step

1 tablespoon vegetable oil or other neutral oil

1½ cup chopped kimchi, plus 2 tablespoons kimchi juice

1 cup sliced onions (about ½ large onion)

1 cup diced zucchini (about 1 small zucchini)

1 cup scrubbed and diced potato (about 2 small red potatoes or ½ russet)

Salt, to taste

4 cups water

1 tablespoon gochujang (optional)

1 teaspoon fish sauce

1 teaspoon sesame oil

2 to 3 tablespoons sliced scallions (1 to 2 scallions)

1 teaspoon sugar, if necessary

There are two main types of the rustic Korean noodle soup called *sujebi*. The non-spicy version, a chicken-based soup with hand-torn noodles made from flour and water, is surprisingly reminiscent of Southern chicken and flat dumplings. This one has a little bit more of a kick, though, simmering kimchi with a dash of fish juice and a heap of hearty vegetables to form a spicy, rich broth—almost like a quick kimchi stew—to go along with the chewy handmade noodles. It's quick but flavorful, and utterly satisfying—my ideal snow-day lunch.

1 *Make the broth while the dumpling dough is resting:* In a large nonstick or well-seasoned cast-iron skillet, heat the oil over medium-high until shimmering. Add the kimchi and onions. Cook, stirring often, until the onions begin to soften and the juices begin to absorb, 2 to 4 minutes.

2 Add the zucchini and potato and season generously with about ½ teaspoon salt. Continue to sauté briefly until zucchini just begins to soften, 1 to 2 more minutes.

3 Transfer the vegetables to a medium saucepan, along with the water, 2 tablespoons kimchi juice, gochujang (if using), fish sauce, and sesame oil. Bring to a boil and let simmer until the potato is nearly cooked but still firm in the center, 10 to 15 minutes.

4 While the broth is simmering, I like to tear the dough into dumplings. Pinch off a tablespoon of dough, then pull this piece in half so that it forms 2 flat pieces. Flatten those pieces to about ¼-inch thick or less, if needed, but otherwise the pieces need not be uniform. Roughly torn edges create a nice texture. Repeat until the dough is gone.

5 Add the dumplings and sliced scallions to the broth. Simmer until the dumplings float and no longer taste floury, 2 to 3 more minutes. If the soup tastes a bit sour, add a teaspoon of sugar. Adjust salt and serve immediately.

an ode to spam

I WAS TWELVE YEARS OLD BEFORE I REALIZED for the first time that Spam wasn't something everyone loved. At summer camp that year, my counselor was a half-Chinese college sophomore. In my whole twelve years of living I had never met a girl who was so cool and self-assured and yet still somewhat like me. We traded stories about our Chinese mothers' cooking, rattling off all the dishes we had in common. *Stir-fried potatoes with mustard greens! Scrambled eggs and tomatoes! Red-cooked pork! Stir-fried green beans with Spam?*

She paused. "Um, no, I don't remember that one," she said at last, tactfully.

Thus came the slow, dawning realization: To me, Spam may have been a delicious, salty, addictive superior to ham, but to almost everyone else I knew, it was abhorrent—nothing more than a clammy pink slab of mystery meat, to be avoided at all costs. Perhaps they would have felt differently had they experienced it, not cold and straight out of the can, but fried in a pan until browned and crackling, crisp on the outside but juicy within, dabbed with oyster sauce and eaten with rice. Or perhaps they wouldn't have. Either way, it was, to my chagrin, anathema.

More than a decade after I'd first discovered my beloved Spam's abiding unpopularity, I was studying in my dorm room in law school, my love of Spam well-hidden (or so I thought), when a classmate of mine sent me a message. I knew him only vaguely. He was half-Korean, and handsome; I had heard he was from Hawaii.

"I heard you like Spam," he typed. My skeleton in the culinary closet! How did he know? I expected him to poke fun, or ask, with incredulity, why. Instead, the next message popped up, friendly and unjudging: "Do you have a *musubi* mold?"

This guy was, of course, my future husband, and it turned out that where he was from, Spam was not reviled but ordinary. He'd grown up eating pan-fried slices of Spam, doused with ketchup and served with a pile of white rice and clouds of scrambled eggs for breakfast; he ate Spam *musubi*—portable, portly versions of overlarge sushi, made by placing Spam on rice and wrapping it up in seaweed—for lunch.

It was a revelation. After hiding my love of Spam for years, I'd met someone who was wholly

indifferent that everyone on the "mainland" hated it, because he'd grown up with it as a part of life. It would be another year before we started dating, but in that conversation I had found my mystery meat soulmate.

"No, I'm so sorry, I don't have a *musubi* mold!" I typed in reply. "I have no idea what that is, actually."

I'm not necessarily saying you should get married to someone just because you share a mutual love for a food most people dislike. But if you do meet someone who happens to be your idea of a dream partner, who happens to fulfill you intellectually and emotionally and share your values, et cetera, but who also happens to have grown up loving a questionably composed, bafflingly shelf-stable canned meat just as much as you did; who introduces you to Spam *musubi,* that triumph of Spam and rice and seaweed; whose idea of a grand morning a few weekends after you've started dating is getting your hands covered in rice by making those *musubi* at home?

Well, in that case, it certainly can't hurt.

BARTER-WORTHY SPAM MUSUBI

Makes 8 or 9 musubi

Musubi are a Hawaii staple, where slices of Spam are fried and cloaked in a lightly flavored sauce, then placed on pressed rice and wrapped in toasty seaweed for a portable, savory snack. You'll find them wrapped tightly in plastic wrap in every 7-Eleven in Hawaii, in lunchboxes at school, in backpacks on hikes. It's not the only way that people in Hawaii enjoy Spam, but it's one of the most popular, and the first time I had one—even the first time my husband described one to me—I was irrevocably in love with them.

According to Andrew, his friend's mother has always made the best *musubi* he's ever had. They were the perfect balance of salty, crispy Spam and just enough sauce, fluffy rice and briny seaweed. In school, "Hyatt's mom's *musubis*" were their own currency, he told me. Hyatt would peddle them at lunch for cash, or use them to barter for coveted snacks. (It has since become my dream to be a mom whose homemade snacks become legal tender.)

To me, a green girlfriend eager to prove her worth, a gauntlet had been thrown. The best *ever*? Every recipe I came across had some variation of Spam, sugar, and soy sauce, with rice and seaweed. How hard could it be to match Hyatt's mom, no matter how legendary her *musubi* were? I was determined to best her.

After that, every weekend for a time saw me elbow-deep in rice, Spam, and nori strips, pressing rice into balls, lining up saucy Spam slices on top, and wrapping them up in seaweed. And yet, with every single recipe I tried, Andrew would just say that it wasn't *quite* it. A bit too salty, he'd say. Too much soy sauce. Or, more mystifying yet, "just not right." After an umpteeth attempt that was "almost but not quite," I finally asked him, in abject defeat, if he'd mind actually emailing her and asking for the legendary recipe.

The email that landed in his inbox just a few hours later was only four lines long. "Fry Spams until brown," she wrote cheerfully. "Add one spoon sugar and some water. Cook until dry, then put on rice balls and wrap with seaweed. Easy!"

I was stunned. No soy sauce! No brown sugar! No way. Refusing to believe that it could be that simple, but with no choice but to try her vaunted recipe, I told my husband we'd be doing a blind taste test. One grain of rice on top of the *musubi* labeled the one made with brown sugar and soy sauce; the one with two grains was made with white sugar and soy sauce. And lastly, three grains, in a dainty triangle, adorned Hyatt's mother's impossibly simple version.

Lo and behold, it was hers that Andrew picked, right away.

(recipe continues)

1 teaspoon vegetable oil or other neutral oil, or as necessary

1 (12-ounce) can Spam, sliced into 8 or 9 pieces

¼ cup water

2 teaspoons soy sauce (see Notes)

2 tablespoons sugar

3 to 4 cups cooked rice, room temperature

3 sheets roasted seaweed (nori), cut into 9 strips about 2 inches wide and 8 inches long

1 Heat a 12-inch nonstick or well-seasoned cast-iron skillet over medium. (If the pan is not nonstick, wait until the pan is hot, then heat a teaspoon or so of oil, just enough to thinly coat the pan.) Add the Spam slices and cook until browned and crisp on the bottom side, 2 to 3 minutes. Flip and cook until the second side is also browned and crisp, an additional 2 to 3 minutes.

2 In a small bowl, whisk together the water and soy sauce. Sprinkle the sugar evenly over the Spam slices, then add the soy sauce mixture. Swirl to evenly distribute, then let the Spam simmer until the liquid is nearly absorbed, 3 to 4 minutes. Remove from the heat and let cool.

3 Meanwhile, prepare your rice and nori strips. When the Spam is cool enough to handle, form the musubi. Place a nori strip on a clean surface or cutting board, with the short end of the nori facing you.

4 *If using a mold:* Place the mold perpendicular to the nori strip in the center of the strip (forming a cross shape) and place a slice of Spam inside the mold. Add about ⅓ to ½ cup of rice, depending on the Spam-to-rice ratio you prefer—we like a bit less rice, and usually use a little over ⅓ cup. Press down firmly on the rice with the mold press, to form a rectangle of rice on top of the Spam. Carefully remove the press and the mold, and fold both ends of the nori strip up and over the rice, sealing with a few stray grains of rice or a bit of water. Turn the musubi seam-side down and set aside while you make the rest. Repeat with the remaining nori strips, Spam, and rice.

5 *If not using a mold:* Place one slice of Spam perpendicular to the nori strip in the center of the strip (forming a cross shape). Wet your hands and pick up ⅓ to ½ cup of rice. Firmly press the rice into a rectangular shape about the size of the Spam, then place on top of the Spam and fold both ends of the nori strip up and over the rice, sealing with a few stray grains of rice or a bit of water. Turn the musubi seam-side down and set aside while you make the rest; repeat with the remaining nori strips, Spam, and rice. Enjoy immediately, or wrap each musubi tightly in plastic wrap for later. If refrigerated, the musubi is best warmed in the microwave for 20 seconds before eating.

NOTES

In a slight departure from the recipe Hyatt's mom so kindly shared, I add just a splash of soy sauce to my Spam. Feel free to omit.

If you like, tuck some egg omelet in between the rice and the Spam (similar to the method in the Ham & Egg Baked Buns, page 35) or a generous sprinkling of *furikake*, a type of Japanese seasoning.

A SAUCIER MUSUBI: TERIYAKI-STYLE

Hyatt's mom's *musubi* is a simpler vision, with just a bit of sauce that clings to the Spam and hints at flavoring the rice. If you want a saltier, saucier, more flavor-forward version, try *teriyaki-style musubi*: Instead of the ¼ cup water, 2 teaspoons soy sauce, and 2 tablespoons sugar called for above, whisk together ⅓ cup soy sauce, ⅓ cup mirin, 3 tablespoons brown sugar (light or dark), and 2 tablespoons sake. Add it to the pan after you've browned the Spam, then let it simmer until the sauce thickens and turns viscous. Remove the Spam slices from the pan, proceed as directed, and serve any sauce that's left over in the pan on the side.

SPICY AHI POKE

Serves 3 or 4

1 pound sushi-grade ahi tuna, fresh or frozen

1 tablespoon soy sauce, or to taste

½ to 1 teaspoon sesame oil, or to taste

¼ cup finely sliced scallions (2 to 3 scallions), plus more for garnish

¼ to ⅓ cup very thinly sliced sweet onion (about ¼ onion; optional)

2 tablespoons Kewpie mayonnaise

1 to 2 tablespoons sriracha

1 to 2 teaspoons masago or tobiko, plus more for garnish

1 teaspoon toasted sesame seeds, for garnish

The first time I had poke was less than an hour after I'd landed at Honolulu International Airport to visit Andrew's family and his home for the first time. Andrew had it waiting, his favorite kind from a Hawaii supermarket chain called Foodland, in the fridge at home. This was before the poke craze that swept the entire country, and back then I had no idea what joy I was about to experience: cool, silky chunks of ahi tuna, layered with flavor and mounded over rice, savory from a soy sauce and sesame oil marinade, but gently spicy from a creamy mayonnaise-based sauce, with pops of flavor and texture from delicate orange fish roe (*masago*), and fresh scallions. It is one of my husband's most beloved foods, and with one bite, it became one of mine, too.

In its most traditional form, poke is usually marinated in a simple combination of soy sauce and and sesame oil, then tossed with scallions, some thinly sliced Maui sweet onion, and topped with sesame seeds, Hawaiian salt, or perhaps some Hawaiian seaweed, *limu*. My husband's favorite is this creamier version, cloaked in a simple mixture of hot sauce and Kewpie mayonnaise after the poke has marinated, and topped with a confetti of *masago* or *tobiko*. The mild heat is a perfect contrast to the fresh, crisp tuna, and the pink sauce will cling seductively to any leftover rice in your bowl for a flavorful ending to your meal.

1 If your tuna is frozen, thaw it briefly by submerging it in very cold water for about 30 minutes. When it's just short of fully thawed, slice it into cubes, about ¾- to 1-inch thick (I tend to go a bit smaller for more flavor).

2 In a medium bowl, combine the tuna, soy sauce, sesame oil, half the scallions, and the onion (if using), and toss until the tuna is well coated. Adjust the soy sauce and sesame oil to your taste—I generally use just enough to coat the tuna thinly. Cover and chill the tuna in the refrigerator for about 30 minutes.

3 Meanwhile, in a small bowl, whisk together the mayonnaise, sriracha, the remaining scallions, and the masago until combined. Add the spicy mayonnaise mixture to the chilled tuna, folding gently until evenly coated. Serve with rice, topped with masago, scallions, and sesame seeds.

NOTES

Take special care to look for sushi- or sashimi-grade tuna when purchasing your fish, and avoid using any that is not clearly labeled as such. Good fish vendors should be able to point you in the right direction.

Masago and *tobiko* are fairly interchangeable—you will generally find *masago* is a bit more affordable, with a less-concentrated flavor, but both will work.

MY MOTHER-IN-LAW'S KOREAN SPICY SHOYU POKE

Serves 3 or 4

This is my mother-in-law's Korean-inspired take on traditional *shoyu* poke. She adds a bit more sesame oil and a smattering of *gochugaru* for a smoky heat; omit the latter, and you have a classic *shoyu* poke.

1 pound sushi-grade ahi tuna, fresh or frozen

2 tablespoons soy sauce, or more to taste

1 to 2 teaspoons sesame oil, or more to taste

2 to 3 teaspoons gochugaru

1 teaspoon toasted sesame seeds, plus more for garnish

¼ cup finely sliced scallions (2 to 3 scallions), plus more for garnish

½ to ¾ cup very thinly sliced sweet onion (about ½ sweet onion)

1 If your tuna is frozen, thaw briefly by submerging it in very cold water for about 30 minutes. When it's just short of fully thawed, slice it into cubes, about ¾ inch or smaller (I tend to go a bit smaller for more flavor).

2 In a medium bowl, combine the tuna, soy sauce, sesame oil, gochugaru, sesame seeds, scallions, and sweet onion and toss until well combined. Serve with rice, topped with more sesame seeds and scallions.

KOREAN MIXED FISH & RICE BOWL
(HWEDUPBAP)

Serves 2

FOR THE
CHO-GOCHUJANG

¼ cup Gochujang Sauce
(page 106)

2 tablespoons rice vinegar

FOR THE HWEDUPBAP

3 cups cooked rice of your
choice (I like short-grain
white rice, but any type
will work)

10 to 12 ounces assorted
sushi-grade fish (I like a
combination of ahi tuna
and salmon)

4 cups chopped red leaf
or romaine lettuce
(about 1 small head)

½ cup julienned carrot
(about 1 carrot)

½ cup julienned Persian
or Kirby cucumber
(1 to 2 cucumbers)

½ cup julienned daikon
radish (about a 2-inch
segment of radish; optional)

¼ cup radish sprouts
or other microgreens
(optional)

¼ cup shredded roasted
seaweed (nori)

3 to 4 tablespoons masago
or tobiko

2 to 3 teaspoons sesame
oil, for garnish

1 tablespoon sesame seeds,
for garnish

I like to think of *hwedupbap* as a summer version of bibimbap—whereas bibimbap is pure belly-warming food, rich with molten yolk and hot from crackling rice, *hwedupbap* is its cool but wonderfully fierce cousin. It bursts with flavors and textures, snappy lettuce and smooth chunks of raw fish against ribbons of carrot and tangy pickled daikon. Underneath it all is a generous portion of fluffy rice for balance, and drizzled on top is the brightly tart but brow-sweatingly hot *cho-gochujang,* a version of *gochujang* sauce cut with vinegar to better complement seafood. It's a dish that's equal parts crisp and silky, spicy and cold, comforting and refreshing. Sassier than Japanese *chirashi* bowls yet quicker than poke, it's not the first way most folks think to enjoy raw fish over rice, but ever since I first had it, it's been one of my most beloved.

---

1 In a small bowl, whisk together the gochujang sauce and rice vinegar to make the cho-gochujang. Set aside.

2 Divide the rice, fish, lettuce, carrot, cucumber, daikon (if using), microgreens, seaweed, and masago between 2 large bowls. Drizzle each bowl with sesame oil and top with sesame seeds. Serve with plenty of cho-gochujang sauce, and enjoy!

GOCHUJANG BUFFALO CHICKEN WRAPS

Makes 4 wraps

While a law school dining hall might not strike you as the most likely source for inspiring cuisine, you'd be hard-pressed to find a buffalo chicken wrap better than the ones I got there. They were perfect in their unapologetic simplicity—fried chicken tenders, fresh red onion, tomato, and iceberg lettuce, swiftly chopped and tucked into a generous tortilla with shredded cheddar, cloaked with plenty of ranch dressing and buffalo sauce, then rolled up neat and tight, with a pickle on the side. No fuss, no frills, and wonderful every time.

I love that wrap because it reminds me that food doesn't have to be complicated to be delicious. This is my nod to it, with just the slightest twist to incorporate *gochujang,* the hot sauce I'm always more likely to have in my own refrigerator than buffalo sauce. There's a splash of vinegar in the *gochujang* sauce to call back the tang of buffalo sauce, but otherwise it adds a smoky-sweet spice to the wrap that is wholly different from its predecessor, yet no less addictive. For even more Korean-inspired heat, sneak in some kimchi-brined spicy chicken (page 40).

Place ½ cup lettuce horizontally across the middle of each tortilla, followed by the chicken, tomato, and red onion. In a small bowl, whisk together the gochujang sauce and rice vinegar until smooth. Drizzle the sauce across each tortilla, followed by the ranch dressing. Fold the ends of the tortillas in over the filling, then roll up widthwise to form a wrap.

2 cups shredded or chopped romaine lettuce (about ½ small head)

4 large (10-inch) flour tortillas

½ pound (about 2 to 3) breaded and fried chicken tenders, diced (or ½ batch kimchi-brined spicy chicken, page 40)

½ cup diced tomato (about 1 small tomato)

¼ cup diced red onion (about ¼ small onion)

1 batch Gochujang Sauce (page 106), or to taste

1 tablespoon rice vinegar

½ cup store-bought ranch dressing, or to taste

DATE NIGHT IN

KOREAN SPICY BARBECUE PORK
(PORK BULGOGI)

Serves 4 to 6

FOR THE MARINADE

½ cup roughly chopped pear or apple (about ½ pear or apple)

⅓ to ½ cup gochujang, depending on how much you like heat (we use the full ½ cup)

⅓ cup packed dark brown sugar

¼ cup roughly chopped onion (about ¼ small onion)

2 tablespoons fish sauce (if unavailable, add an extra tablespoon soy sauce; optional)

2 tablespoons rice cooking wine

2 tablespoons minced garlic (4 to 6 cloves)

1 tablespoon soy sauce

1 tablespoon sesame oil

1 teaspoon finely grated ginger root

⅛ teaspoon black pepper

(ingredients continue)

Growing up in a town in the South meant that I could remember when the first restaurants featuring almost every kind of "different" (to us) cuisine came to our little city, and the first time I ever tried those wonderful foods. A big bowl of deeply flavorful pho from a Vietnamese restaurant; my first sweet-savory pad thai, with tangles of chewy rice noodles flecked with peanut; creamy orange chicken tikka masala piled atop fluffy jasmine rice.

The first Korean restaurant in our town was a tiny joint, one of those order-at-the-counter restaurants with room for only a few tables, helmed by a small, beaming woman. This cheerful owner was the one who first introduced my family to pork bulgogi, a mound of fiery red pork that was then known to me only as "Korean spicy barbecue pork." Back then it was almost always too spicy for me, but it was still so addictive that, even as my brow broke out in a sweat from the spice, I couldn't stop eating it. I've been in love with it ever since.

Pork bulgogi is simultaneously smoky-hot and sharp from the red pepper paste yet deliciously sweet and savory underneath, an embodiment of the thing I most love about Korean food—its wholehearted embrace of the ability of sweetness to enhance umami and spice. I still miss that little Korean restaurant in my hometown, but with the right ingredients at home, I'm transported back there every time I make this in my own kitchen.

---

1 Combine the marinade ingredients in a blender or food processor and whizz until puréed and as smooth as you can get it, 1 to 2 minutes. Combine with the pork, onion, and scallions in a large Ziploc freezer bag or a shallow dish, massaging to ensure every piece is evenly coated. Marinate in the refrigerator for at least 30 minutes, ideally 2 to 3 hours or overnight. You can also freeze it at this point for a quick meal down the road.

(recipe continues)

FOR THE REST

2 pounds pork butt, neck, or shoulder, thinly sliced

¾ cup sliced onion (the rest of the onion, from above)

¼ cup sliced scallions (2 to 3 scallions), plus more for serving

1 to 2 tablespoons vegetable oil or other neutral oil

Gochujang, to taste (optional)

Soy sauce, to taste (optional)

Brown sugar, light or dark, to taste (optional)

1 to 2 tablespoons toasted sesame seeds, for serving

Cooked rice, for serving

2 In a large skillet (preferably cast-iron), heat 1 to 2 tablespoons vegetable oil over medium-high until shimmering. Add about a third of the pork, vegetables, and marinade into the pan, leaving plenty of room for the pork. Cook, stirring infrequently, until marinade begins to evaporate and charred, caramelized bits begin to form at the edges of the pan, 7 to 8 minutes. Taste the pork and add more gochujang, soy sauce, or brown sugar, if needed.

3 Transfer the pork to a serving plate (I like to use stove-safe cast-iron baking dishes that I can keep warm on another burner), and wipe out any particularly burnt bits. Repeat with the second and third batches, turning the heat down to medium if the pork starts to burn. The caramelization is the best part—as long as the pan isn't too blackened, just keep cooking without bothering to wash it out completely. Serve immediately, with sesame seeds and extra scallions on top, and rice on the side.

SKILLET "DOLSOT" BIBIMBAP

Serves 6

If I ever had to choose one meal to eat for the rest of my life, bibimbap would be it. It's so full of myriad textures and flavors that it almost can't be considered one dish—there's crunch from the vegetables and crispy nori, savoriness from the bulgogi and a subtle sweetness from the carrots and onions, and then the decadent buttery egg yolk and *gochujang* sauce to tie it all together into a spicy package.

Dolsot bibimbap is made by slicking sesame oil in the bottom of a hot, sizzling stone bowl (a *dolsot*) and piling white rice atop it, so that the bottom forms a crisp, flavorful crust by the time you stir it up with all your fixings. With limited space in my tiny Brooklyn apartment and little reason to justify buying more single-use kitchen items, I took to making the *dolsot*-esque crust in my workhorse cast-iron skillet. It's the perfect way to add a little something extra to your bibimbap without hunting down a specialty item at your nearest Korean supermarket, and when making bibimbap for a crowd, the ease can't be beat.

---

1 *To cook the vegetables, sauté each type separately:* In a large nonstick skillet, heat a tablespoon or so vegetable oil over medium-high. Add the vegetable, then season generously with salt and pepper and cook, stirring, until tender. Carrots will take about 3 to 4 minutes, zucchini 1 to 2 minutes, onions 5 to 7 minutes, and mushrooms 5 to 7 minutes. You can add a touch of soy sauce to the mushrooms, if you like. When each vegetable is done, remove and sprinkle with 1 to 2 teaspoons sesame seeds, then set aside.

2 Bring a large pot of water to a boil. Add the spinach and blanch briefly until bright green and soft, 30 seconds or less. Drain and rinse with cold water to stop the cooking, then toss the spinach with 1 tablespoon garlic, 1 to 2 tablespoons sesame oil, 2 teaspoons sesame seeds, 1 teaspoon soy sauce, salt, and pepper. Taste and adjust seasonings as needed. Set aside.

(recipe continues)

---

4 to 6 tablespoons vegetable oil or other neutral oil, or more as needed

2 cups julienned carrots (about 4 medium carrots)

2 cups julienned zucchini (2 to 4 zucchini)

2 cups thinly sliced onion (1 to 2 onions)

2 cups thinly sliced shiitake mushrooms (4 to 5 mushrooms)

Salt and black pepper, to taste

1 teaspoon soy sauce, or more to taste

3 to 4 teaspoons toasted sesame seeds, divided

5 to 6 cups packed torn spinach leaves

1 tablespoon minced garlic (2 to 3 cloves)

2 to 4 tablespoons sesame oil, divided

8 to 10 cups cooked rice

4 to 6 large eggs (1 per person)

1 batch beef bulgogi (page 109)

Shredded roasted seaweed (nori), for serving

1 batch Gochujang Sauce (page 106), for serving

3 Finally, in a large cast-iron skillet, heat 1 to 2 tablespoons sesame oil over low. When the oil is hot, add the rice to the skillet and spread gently into an even layer. Cook, without stirring, for about 15 minutes, letting the rice crackle very gently, until the bottom layer of rice forms a golden, crisp crust.

4 The very last thing I like to do is fry the eggs, generally as the rice is cooking and we are getting ready to eat. I find that folks are usually pretty evenly divided between sunny-side-up and over-easy eggs for bibimbap, though almost everyone likes them a little bit runny inside. For sunny-side up, in a medium nonstick skillet, heat 1 tablespoon of vegetable oil over medium-low. Crack the eggs gently into the skillet and cook, without moving them, until the whites are set and opaque, 1 to 2 minutes. For over easy, gently flip the eggs after 1 minute of cooking (the whites can still be slightly translucent) and cook until the whites are set but the yolks are still soft, another 30 seconds or so.

5 Divide the rice between 6 large, shallow bowls, followed by the beef bulgogi, vegetables, eggs, and a handful of roasted seaweed on top. Serve with gochujang sauce on top or on the side for guests to drizzle to their liking.

NOTES

If you find you have generous amounts of leftovers, it all freezes well. Pre-assemble any leftover bowls (minus the eggs) and freeze them for to-go lunches later on.

If you have access to a Korean supermarket, there are plenty of other goodies you can add to bibimbap. Fernbrake (or *gosari*) is one; it may need to be soaked for several hours, then blanched as the spinach is. Soybean or mung bean sprouts are one of our favorites for the texture they add. To prepare the sprouts, blanch them until soft, about 10 minutes, then rinse in cold water and toss with 2 teaspoons sesame oil, 2 teaspoons *gochugaru,* 1 teaspoon soy sauce, salt and black pepper to taste, and 2 teaspoons sesame seeds. Taste and adjust the seasonings as needed, and use with the rest of the vegetables.

GOCHUJANG SAUCE
(FOR BIBIMBAP, BUFFALO CHICKEN WRAPS, AND HWEDUPBAP)

Makes about 1 cup

½ cup gochujang

2 tablespoons sesame oil

2 tablespoons soy sauce, or to taste

2 tablespoons sugar or honey

1 tablespoon toasted sesame seeds

1 teaspoon minced garlic (1 clove; optional)

1 to 2 teaspoons water, or as needed for thinning (optional)

Spicy and sweet, smoky and savory, tangy and pungent, this sauce is incredibly flavorful and might very well be my favorite condiment in existence. I always end up adding more and more until I've gone too far and my mouth is on fire. It's that good—I'm convinced you could put it on anything and it would be delicious. The amounts here are more guidelines than rules, and you'll find that they're happily forgiving. More often than not, I freehand the ingredients as I go, and the sauce has never once been anything but perfect.

In a small bowl, whisk the gochujang, sesame oil, soy sauce, sugar, sesame seeds, and garlic (if using) until smooth. Add water as needed to thin the sauce to your desired consistency. The sauce will keep for 1 to 2 weeks in the refrigerator.

KOREAN BARBECUE BEEF
(BEEF BULGOGI)

Serves 4 as a main, or 6 to 8 in bibimbap (see page 103)

Where pork bulgogi is sassy, loud, and spicy, beef bulgogi is its quiet companion, sweeter and deliciously savory. The beef is sliced thin and tenderized in a slow marinade in soy sauce, sesame oil, and a little brown sugar, so that it cooks up flavorful and tender. Alongside jammy onions, carrots, and earthy mushrooms, it is a full meal on its own over fluffy white rice, but does double duty in Skillet "Dolsot" Bibimbap (page 103), *japchae, kimbap,* and all sorts of other goodies. It may be quieter, but frequently it is the true star of the show.

1 Combine the marinade ingredients in a blender or food processor and whizz until puréed and as smooth as you can get it, 1 to 2 minutes. Combine with the beef, mushrooms, onion, and scallions in a large Ziploc freezer bag or a shallow dish, and marinate in the refrigerator for at least 30 minutes, ideally 2 to 3 hours or overnight. You can also freeze it at this point for a quick meal down the road.

2 In a large, skillet (preferably cast-iron), heat 1 to 2 tablespoons vegetable oil over medium-high until shimmering. Add about a third of the beef, vegetables, and marinade into the pan, leaving plenty of room for the beef to cook. Cook, stirring infrequently, for 6 to 8 minutes, until marinade begins to evaporate and caramelized bits begin to form at the edges of the pan. Taste the beef and add more soy sauce and brown sugar, if needed.

3 Once done, transfer the beef to a serving plate (I like to use stove-safe cast-iron baking dishes that I can keep warm on another burner), and wipe out any particularly burnt bits. Repeat with the second and third batches, turning the heat down to medium if the beef starts to burn. The caramelization is the best part—as long as the pan isn't too blackened, just keep cooking without bothering to wash out the pan completely. Serve immediately, with sesame seeds and extra scallions on top, and rice on the side.

NOTES

If you have access to a Korean supermarket, look for pre-sliced bulgogi meat. Otherwise, partially freeze the beef to make for easier, more precise slicing, and try to slice the meat about ⅛-inch thick or thinner, if you can.

FOR THE MARINADE

½ cup roughly chopped pear or apple (about ½ pear or apple)

¼ cup roughly chopped onion (about ¼ small onion)

⅓ cup soy sauce, or to taste

3 tablespoons dark brown sugar

2 tablespoons minced garlic (4 to 6 cloves)

1 tablespoon sesame oil

½ teaspoon gochugaru or crushed red pepper flakes

⅛ teaspoon black pepper

FOR THE BEEF

1 to 2 tablespoons vegetable oil or other neutral oil

1 pound very thinly sliced boneless beef short rib, rib eye, or sirloin

¾ cup sliced onion (the rest of the small onion, from above)

½ cup sliced mushrooms of your choice (optional)

¼ cup sliced scallions (2 to 3 scallions), plus more for serving

Soy sauce, to taste (optional)

Dark brown sugar, to taste (optional)

2 tablespoons toasted sesame seeds, for serving

Cooked rice, for serving

two red bowls, and a basement on irving street

DURING OUR LAST SEMESTER OF LAW SCHOOL, Andrew lived in an apartment in the basement of a building just outside Harvard Square. The apartment didn't seem to have heat—or, if it did, then the building had decidedly little insulation—and his bedroom was covered, for some reason, in a bubbly linoleum. Windows tucked up high near the ceiling let in pale strips of sunshine and a view of people's boots as they hustled by on the Cambridge sidewalks. Exposed pipes ran the length of the apartment and banged ominously when anyone showered.

Andrew, rather than being fazed by this, was triumphant that he'd landed such a cheap apartment. After all, it wasn't as though he needed much: His mattress sat directly on the floor of his bedroom, and the narrow kitchen boasted one pan, a coffeemaker, and a George Foreman grill.

Yet that chilly basement apartment became the place we spent most of our time the semester before we graduated. I brought a space heater, which worked bravely in about a ten-foot radius but no farther; Andrew ordered a metal bed frame on Amazon for $49. One day, he brought me into the kitchen to show me two cheerful, cherry-red plastic bowls, which he told me he'd bought from, of all places, a hardware store down the street. Paper plates, begone! We were well on our way to making 28 Irving Street a respectable dwelling.

We woke up in the mornings to the crunch of footsteps on snow and the automated messages of street cleaners as they whirred just above our heads, and after class we sat on an extra-squashy couch in the living room to study, eating dinner out of our new red bowls (often with our coats on).

Though we'd been dating for a little while, the semester we spent in the basement on Irving Street was the time we first learned to live together. The things I appreciated about my boyfriend—his serious intelligence, a quiet stoicism in public that masked a goofy sense of humor and a tender kindness in private, his interest in the same nerdy things that I'd loved as a kid—I now began to understand in practice.

As we went back and forth to class together, studied and did our reading and met our friends for drinks on glacial Cambridge winter nights, Irving Street was where I learned my future husband was a night owl who needed dismayingly little sleep (while I, on the other hand, viewed anything less than eight hours a night to be an utter calamity). He liked his coffee black and his steak at any level of doneness, but always with his mom's sesame oil dipping sauce, *gireumjang* (page 116); I discovered that he liked to make things, after he disappeared to a woodworking shop every weekend for a month in order to produce a tiny wooden chest, in reference to our favorite video game, for my Valentine's Day gift.

It was where, when Hurricane Nemo arrived overnight and we awoke to find our narrow windows totally obscured by blue-white snow, I was gleeful to find I wasn't the only one whose idea of a perfect weekend was working my way through a heaping wok-ful of orange kimchi fried rice (page 113), re-watching *Star Wars* from start to finish, and never once changing out of my pajamas.

And, in April 2013, a month before we graduated, the living room was where I took my first grainy iPhone photos of bibimbap in our two hardware-store bowls and posted them to a Word-Press blog I tentatively titled—after a brief internal debate between the bowls and two blue plates we'd subsequently acquired—*Two Red Bowls.*

Every apartment we've lived in after Irving has been, if not nicer, significantly warmer, higher off the ground, and with far less questionable flooring. The sunshine streaming through our California living room makes it hard to believe that I ever spent four months shivering in a dark, snowed-in apartment, reading patent law notes with my gloves on. And yet we bring up our time there more often than either of us would have expected at the time, smiling at the thought of playing video games on the floor, pipes banging like an engine backfiring, or a kitchen that had only one pan and two nested red bowls. It just goes to show, perhaps, that—while a bed frame and working heat definitely help—all you need to make the greatest of homes is one pan, a good batch of kimchi fried rice, and a really great someone to share it with.

FRIDAY NIGHT KIMCHI FRIED RICE

Serves 4 to 6

This might just be my husband's favorite dish ever, one that I think he could eat all day, every day, ad infinitum. When done well, kimchi fried rice is impossibly flavorful and full of texture, simultaneously crunchy from the kimchi but smooth and creamy from the egg yolk, soft for some bites but crisp for others, just spicy enough, and laced with savory comfort.

This recipe largely comes from my mother-in-law, but I've tweaked it slightly over time. It's best with good, quality kimchi that is on its last legs in the fridge, very well-fermented and funky. After playing with the method, I've eventually found that cooking the kimchi the longest, and with its liquid, is the best way to concentrate all that spicy, funky flavor into the umami bomb it should be. For us, this is the best kind of home-cooked food—easy but comforting, full of childhood memories, the perfect Friday night treat after a long work week.

---

1 Beat the eggs with ¼ teaspoon salt. In a large wok or skillet, heat a few teaspoons vegetable oil over medium-high and swirl to evenly coat the wok. When the oil is shimmering, add the eggs and scramble to your liking; I like to scramble them as I do for Chinese Scrambled Eggs & Tomatoes (page 195). I find that breaking the eggs into smaller pieces makes for more flavorful fried rice. Remove from the wok and set aside.

2 Heat another teaspoon or so of oil over medium and swirl to evenly coat the wok. Add the kimchi and kimchi liquid. Let the kimchi cook, stirring occasionally, until parts of the kimchi begin to dry out and turn dark orange and the liquid begins to concentrate, 4 to 5 minutes. Remove from the heat, transfer the kimchi to a bowl, and rinse out the wok.

3 Again, heat a few teaspoons of oil in the wok over medium. Add the onion and garlic, season with salt, and cook, stirring frequently, until the onion begins to soften, 3 to 4 minutes. Return the cooked egg and fried kimchi to the wok, then add the Spam. Stir until combined.

(recipe continues)

4 large eggs, plus 1 whole egg per person for frying

¼ teaspoon salt, plus more for seasoning

1 tablespoon vegetable oil or other neutral oil, or as needed

4 cups well-fermented kimchi, chopped and drained (reserve the liquid!), plus 2 tablespoons kimchi liquid

1 large onion, diced (about 2 cups)

2 tablespoons minced garlic (4 to 6 cloves)

1 (12-ounce) can Spam or Spam Lite, diced

5 to 6 cups cooked rice (see Notes)

2 to 3 teaspoons sesame oil, to taste

1 tablespoon gochujang

Shredded nori, for garnish (optional)

4 Add the rice and use a silicone spatula or wooden spoon to break it up vigorously until fully mixed together. (This will take some arm strength and sweat, but the good news is that it always makes me feel justified in eating an extra bowl.)

5 Add the sesame oil and gochujang and continue to toss until thoroughly incorporated. Season with additional salt as desired, then turn the heat to its lowest setting and let the rice continue to cook, without stirring, to let the bottom layer crisp up while you prepare the eggs to go on top. You might want to check the rice after about 5 minutes or so to make sure it's not browning too much.

6 Meanwhile, in a medium nonstick skillet, heat 1 tablespoon of vegetable oil over medium-low. For sunny-side up eggs, crack the eggs gently into the skillet and cook, without moving them, until the whites are set and opaque, 1 to 2 minutes. For over easy, gently flip the eggs after 1 minute of cooking (the whites can still be slightly translucent) and cook until the whites are set but the yolks are still soft, another 30 seconds or so. Either way, I like to leave the egg yolk runny—the rice tastes wonderfully creamy with the yolk mixed in. It's my favorite part.

7 Divide the fried rice into bowls, top with the fried eggs, and garnish with shredded nori, if desired. Enjoy immediately. Leftovers will keep in the fridge for up to 1 week, and can be enjoyed hot or cold, though we've never once had it last that long. In fact, my husband likes it straight from the fridge with ketchup, late at night.

NOTES

As with the Blank Canvas Chinese Fried Rice (page 60), I have not found using refrigerated, day-old rice to be necessary. Using freshly cooked rice will work fine—just make sure to use a bit less water than usual when cooking your rice if you're concerned about mushiness.

SESAME SALT & PEPPER STEAK
(WITH GIREUMJANG)

Serves 2

All it takes is the smell of sesame oil for my husband to come wandering into the kitchen. Even a small amount can fill up the whole room, piercing and immediately recognizable, yet the smell is a round, mellow one, like a warm, booming laugh. "Something smells *good*," Andrew will inevitably say, perking up with Pavlovian interest. "When do we eat?"

When something can rouse an appetite so powerfully all on its own, it needs very little else to become a good meal, and *gireumjang*, a sandy-textured dipping sauce made from nothing more than sesame oil, salt, and black pepper, is proof positive of this. Nutty and toasty, punched up from the salt and warm from the black pepper, *gireumjang* is typically served with thin slices of barbecued pork belly, or *samgyeopsal*, but my mother-in-law also favors serving it with strips of sirloin steak. The latter, smoky from a quick sear in a good cast-iron pan, is my favorite.

1 pound boneless rib eye, New York strip, or top sirloin steak, about 1-inch thick

¼ teaspoon salt, or to taste

¼ teaspoon black pepper, or to taste

1 tablespoon vegetable oil or other neutral oil

1 batch Gireumjang (page 116)

---

1 Season the steak generously with salt and pepper on both sides. If the steak is cold, let it rest until it comes close to room temperature, 30 minutes to 1 hour.

2 In a 10- or 12-inch cast-iron pan or other thick-bottomed skillet, heat a slick of vegetable oil over high until shimmering and very hot. Add the steak and let sizzle energetically for 2 to 3 minutes, until a nice brown crust forms on the bottom side. Flip and cook for an additional 1 to 3 minutes, until the steak reaches your desired doneness. An instant-read thermometer is tremendously useful for checking doneness—medium-rare will read between 130°F to 140°F, medium will read 140°F to 150°F, and medium-well 150°F to 155°F. If you don't have a thermometer, just use a spatula to press lightly on the center of the steak. At medium-rare, the steak will feel like your cheek, mostly soft but with some structure; at medium, the steak will feel like the fleshy part of your chin, still soft but with more resistance; at medium-well, it will feel like your forehead between your brows, fairly firm.

(recipe continues)

3 Remove the steak from the heat and let rest for 5 to 10 minutes to let the juices distribute. Meanwhile, make the gireumjang if you haven't already. Slice the steak and serve with gireumjang drizzled over top or on the side as a dipping sauce.

---

korean salt & pepper sesame sauce (gireumjang)

MAKES ABOUT ¼ CUP

1 tablespoon salt

1½ teaspoons black pepper

3 tablespoons sesame oil

Mix together the salt and pepper in a small bowl. Stir in the sesame oil until incorporated. Enjoy, or refrigerate until needed. The sauce will keep for several weeks.

GARLIC, GINGER & SOY SALMON EN PAPILLOTE

Serves 2

2 (8-ounce) salmon fillets

1½ inches (about ¾ ounce) ginger root, sliced

6 to 8 garlic cloves, peeled and smashed

⅓ cup chopped scallions (about 3 scallions)

⅓ cup soy sauce

¼ cup packed dark brown sugar

3 tablespoons Shaoxing rice wine, dry sherry, or sake

Cooked rice, for serving

Garlicky Bok Choy (page 192) or other cooked vegetables, for serving

In those early days of law school, re-creating all my childhood meals in a kitchen far from home, one of the first recipes I begged my mother to teach me was her pan-seared salmon. Cooked sizzling in a smoking wok, her salmon was silky and flavorful, with a fantastically crisp soy-caramelized skin. But it could be a bit of an endeavor, requiring constant attention and more than a little sweat and labor over a spitting wok. Over the years, looking for a quicker, more hands-off alternative, I've resorted to a little help from the French to keep this dish manageable but still date-night special. Cooking fish *en papillote*, or in parchment, is an elegant term for a very simple concept. Sealing the fish in parchment paper (or foil, if you prefer) and steaming it nice and slow yields a tender, buttery fish with no fuss, almost no hands-on time, and no sticky, blackened wok to clean up. To drive home the flavor, I make a reduction from some of the marinade to drizzle on top, for a beautifully flavorful fish that soaks up all the sweet and salty flavors from soy sauce, brown sugar, garlic, ginger, and scallions, and tastes just like my mother makes.

1 *Up to 1 day ahead, or at least 30 minutes in advance:* Place the salmon in a large Ziploc bag or shallow baking dish. Mix together the ginger, garlic, scallions, soy sauce, brown sugar, and rice wine, and pour over the salmon. Seal airtight and marinate in the refrigerator for at least 30 minutes, ideally 2 to 3 hours or up to 1 day in advance.

2 *When ready to cook:* Preheat the oven to 325°F. Take a large piece of parchment paper or foil and fold it in half. It should be larger than the salmon by at least 3 to 4 inches on each side. (The larger it is, the easier it is to fold.) Cut the parchment so that it forms a heart shape when unfolded.

3 Unfold the parchment and place a salmon fillet along the crease, along with a third of the ginger, garlic, and scallions from the marinade. Drizzle a tablespoon or two of the marinade liquid over the fish, then fold the parchment over the fillet and pleat the edges shut, starting with the rounded side of the heart. Pleat the end tightly and twist to seal. (Foil will seal more easily, if you find parchment difficult to work with. Either way, don't fret—an airtight seal is ideal but by no means necessary.)

4 Repeat with the second salmon fillet, reserving the remaining marinade, ginger, garlic, and scallions for the sauce.

5 Bake the fish on a rimmed baking sheet until a fork inserted into the thickest part of the salmon meets with no resistance and the salmon flakes easily, 15 to 20 minutes, longer for a larger piece of fish. It's hard to overcook the salmon using this method, so if you're unsure about the cooking time, just let it go on the slightly longer side. Alternatively, use an instant-read meat thermometer to check the fish for doneness—it should read 125°F in the very thickest part of the fish if using farm-raised salmon, or 120°F if using wild salmon.

6 During the last 5 minutes of baking, pour the reserved marinade, ginger, garlic, and scallions into a small saucepan and turn the heat to medium-high. Cook, stirring frequently, until the marinade bubbles and thickens slightly, 3 to 4 minutes. If desired, adjust the sauce to taste with more soy sauce and brown sugar. Serve over the fish or on the side, with plenty of rice and a vegetable side (I like Garlicky Bok Choy, page 192, or broccoli).

PAPPARDELLE WITH LAMB RAGÙ

Serves 6 to 8

2 pounds lamb shank
(about 2 shanks; see Notes)

Salt and black pepper,
to taste

2 tablespoons olive oil

2 cups diced onion
(1 to 2 onions)

1 tablespoon minced garlic
(3 to 4 cloves)

1 cup red wine

1 (28-ounce) can crushed
tomatoes

½ cup diced carrot
(about 1 carrot)

¼ cup fresh oregano
leaves, chopped

2 tablespoons finely
minced rosemary leaves

1 tablespoon chili garlic
paste (1 to 2 teaspoons
sriracha also works)

4 cups shredded kale leaves
(see Notes)

2 pounds dried or 3 pounds
fresh pappardelle

Shaved Parmesan cheese,
for serving

NOTES

Feel free to use pork
shoulder in place of
the lamb, if preferred.
Collard greens also
work wonderfully here
in place of the kale.

This marvelous *ragù* is inspired by the ingenious pork shoulder *ragù* in *Dinner: A Love Story* by Jenny Rosenstrach and her husband Andy Ward, which is more mind-blowingly delicious than any recipe so simple and so hands-off has any right to be. I've replaced the pork with lamb for an earthy flavor and thrown in some hearty greens for texture, but the elegant simplicity of their recipe remains. Combine the hunks of meat with aromatics, tomatoes, and a healthy glug of wine, pop it into the oven, and walk away. Three hours later, what you get is deeply flavorful and tender, falling off the bone, and ready to be melded together into one beautifully rich sauce. I like it best over bouncy, bright-yellow egg pappardelle, but it works well with any pasta of your choice.

---

1 Preheat the oven to 300°F. Season the lamb shanks generously with salt and pepper (I use about 1 teaspoon salt and ½ teaspoon pepper). Set aside.

2 In a large Dutch oven, heat the oil over medium-high until shimmering. Add the onions and garlic, season with salt and pepper, reduce the heat to medium, and cook, stirring often, until the onions just begin to soften, 1 to 2 minutes. Add the lamb shanks, wine, tomatoes, carrot, oregano, rosemary, and chili garlic paste, and give it all a good stir. Reduce the heat to low and simmer for 3 to 4 minutes, then cover and place in the oven.

3 Braise for 3 to 4 hours, turning the shanks every hour. If the liquid starts to cook dry, add water, 1 cup at a time, enough to keep the liquid about halfway up the lamb. By the end of the cooking time, the meat should be falling off the shanks.

4 Remove the pot from the oven and use tongs to transfer the shanks to a bowl or a cutting board. Use forks to pull the meat off the bone and shred it finely, then return the shredded meat to the pot and stir. Place over medium-low heat and add the kale. Cook until the kale is tender, 15 to 20 minutes.

5 Meanwhile, bring a large pot of water to a boil for the pasta. Cook the pasta according to package directions. Divide the cooked pasta among 6 to 8 bowls, top with the ragù, and serve with plenty of shaved Parmesan.

BULGOGI BURGERS

Serves 4

I first thought of trying a bulgogi-marinated burger years ago, but it fell by the wayside until we tasted something almost identical at an Asian-inspired burger joint in Sawtelle. They marinated their beef patties in a sweet soy concoction, and after my first taste I couldn't fathom why *all* burgers weren't marinated before cooking them. I came up with this recipe soon after. The bulgogi marinade infuses the burger patty with an addictive umami-laced sweetness; paired with a rich, dripping, sunny-side-up egg, crispy fried shallots, and a spicy *gochujang* mayonnaise, it's by far the most flavorful burger I've ever made.

---

1 *The night before, or at least 30 minutes in advance:* Divide the beef into 4 equal balls, about 2½ inches in diameter. Place them in a shallow baking dish or a 1-quart Ziploc bag. Mix the soy sauce, scallions, brown sugar, garlic, sesame oil, gochugaru, and black pepper in a small bowl until well combined. Pour over the ground beef and make sure it is well distributed around the beef. Do not mix it in. Let the beef marinate in the refrigerator for at least 30 minutes, ideally 2 to 3 hours or overnight. Turn the beef once or twice to make sure all sides are thoroughly coated in the marinade.

2 *The day of:* Whisk together the mayonnaise and gochujang until well combined; set aside.

3 Transfer the beef balls from the marinade to a baking sheet and place in the freezer for no longer than 15 minutes. Briefly freezing the beef allows a nice brown crust to form on the patty without it cooking too quickly.

4 *While the burgers are in the freezer, toast the buns:* Heat a 10- or 12-inch cast-iron skillet over medium. Split open 2 of the potato rolls, brush shallot oil over the cut sides, then place them cut-side down in the skillet. Cook until nicely toasted, then transfer to a platter. Repeat with the remaining rolls. Set aside.

(recipe continues)

FOR THE BEEF

1 pound good-quality ground beef, preferably with an 80/20 fat ratio

⅓ cup soy sauce

¼ cup sliced scallions (2 to 3 scallions)

3 tablespoons dark brown sugar

2 tablespoons minced garlic (4 to 6 cloves)

1 tablespoon sesame oil

¼ teaspoon gochugaru or crushed red pepper flakes

⅛ teaspoon black pepper

FOR THE GOCHUJANG MAYONNAISE

½ cup mayonnaise

1 tablespoon gochujang (sriracha also works in a pinch)

FOR THE BURGERS

4 potato rolls (preferably Martin's brand) or hamburger buns (or use Our Favorite Enriched Bread, shaped into buns)

¼ cup shallot oil (from Crispy Fried Shallots, recipe follows) or melted unsalted butter, or more as needed, divided

4 large eggs

½ cup Crispy Fried Shallots (recipe follows)

½ cup thinly sliced scallions (3 to 4 scallions)

5 Wipe out the skillet, then return it to high heat. Add 1 to 2 tablespoons shallot oil and swirl until it evenly coats the pan. Heat until very hot, just shy of smoking. (You may want to open your windows if you can!) Place 2 beef balls into the skillet, leaving plenty of room between, and smash them down with the back of a large spatula until they're flattened into a patty about an inch larger than you'd like the final burger to be. Craggy, uneven edges are good here. Cook for about 2 minutes without moving the patties, then flip and cook on the other side for an additional 1 to 2 minutes. The patties should be very browned with dark, nearly burnt bits. Remove and repeat with another tablespoon of shallot oil and the remaining beef balls.

6 In a large nonstick skillet (or in the same cast-iron skillet, wiped clean), heat 1 tablespoon of shallot oil over medium. Fry the eggs sunny-side up or over easy (see page 105).

7 Layer each bun bottom with plenty of gochujang mayonnaise, the beef patties, an egg, some crispy fried shallots, and sliced scallions. Add the bun tops and serve immediately.

---

crispy fried shallots

MAKES ½ TO ¾ CUP FRIED SHALLOTS AND 1 CUP SHALLOT OIL

1½ cups very thinly sliced shallots (3 to 4 shallots)

1 cup vegetable oil or other neutral oil

1 Use a paper towel to blot out any excess moisture from the shallots. Line a rimmed baking sheet with 2 layers of paper towels. Set a large metal colander over a heatproof bowl.

2 Place the oil and the shallots in a large saucepan or skillet over medium-high heat. When the shallots begin to bubble, reduce heat to medium-low. Let the shallots bubble gently, stirring occasionally to prevent any hot spots, until golden-brown. This will take a good long while, 10 to 15 minutes, but will ensure all the shallots brown up evenly. Pour the shallots into the prepared colander, letting the oil drain into the bowl below. Spread the shallots over the paper towel–lined baking sheet to drain completely. Use immediately and store leftovers in the freezer. Reserve the oil for use in practically anything savory (most of the sautéed vegetables in this book and the fried rice are a great start).

KIMCHI CHICKEN QUESADILLAS

Makes 4 quesadillas

After my discovery of the perfect marriage between kimchi and cheese, there was a time when I wanted to combine them in everything—macaroni and cheese, omelet, nachos, you name it. After a Kimchi Egg & Cheese (page 57), this was the next best combination to arise out of my obsession. Spicy, tangy kimchi is a natural stand-in for salsa, and couldn't be better suited to give that much-needed lift to the decadence of cheese, meat, and tortillas. Here, kimchi does double-duty in the quesadillas themselves and in the sour cream, where it adds the perfect bit of pique to a quick and hearty lunch.

---

1 In a medium skillet, heat 1 to 2 teaspoons oil over medium-high until shimmering. Season the chicken breast generously with salt and pepper on each side (I use about ¼ teaspoon of each) and add to the skillet; it should sizzle on contact. Cook on one side until golden brown, 2 to 3 minutes; flip and cook until the second side is also golden brown, an additional 2 to 3 minutes. Turn off the heat and cover the pan; let sit, without touching, until the chicken is cooked through, about 6 minutes. Transfer the chicken to a cutting board and dice.

2 Meanwhile, in a large skillet, heat 1 to 2 teaspoons of oil over medium-high until shimmering. Add the kimchi and sauté just until hot and kimchi liquid has been absorbed a bit, 2 to 3 minutes. Transfer to a bowl and wipe out the skillet.

3 Return the skillet to the heat and add just enough oil to coat the pan. Add a tortilla to the pan. On half of the tortilla, layer a handful (about ¼ cup) Monterey Jack, a generous sprinkling (about 2 tablespoons) of cheddar, a quarter of the chicken, and 3 to 4 tablespoons of the sautéed kimchi. Fold the tortilla up over the filling. When the bottom turns a nice golden brown, after 2 to 3 minutes or so, flip and let the other side cook until golden brown, an additional 1 to 2 minutes.

4 Repeat with the remaining tortillas and filling ingredients. To serve, whisk together the remaining ¼ cup kimchi and the sour cream to make a dipping sauce, and sprinkle cilantro and scallions on top, if desired. Enjoy immediately.

FOR THE QUESADILLAS

2 to 4 teaspoons vegetable oil or other neutral oil, or more as needed, divided

1 (5- to 6-ounce) boneless, skinless chicken breast

Salt and black pepper, to taste

1 cup chopped kimchi

4 (8-inch) flour or corn tortillas

1 cup (3 to 4 ounces) shredded Monterey Jack cheese

½ cup (1 to 2 ounces) shredded cheddar cheese

FOR SERVING

¼ cup finely chopped kimchi

½ cup sour cream

½ cup chopped cilantro, for serving (optional)

½ cup chopped scallions, for serving (optional)

CELEBRATIONS
& GATHERINGS

the universal language of dish-washing

THE FIRST TIME I MET THE KOREAN SIDE OF MY future husband's extended family was at Christmas. It was the Ha annual Christmas party, and when the cavalry arrived, it took all of twenty minutes for my future mother-in-law's kitchen to go from quiet serenity to all-out—albeit highly organized—chaos. One auntie arrived bearing a tub the size of a small whale, filled to the brim with Korean short ribs, or *galbi*, swimming in marinade; another auntie exchanged her outside shoes for slippers while balancing a basket of salt-and-pepper shrimp under one arm; and a third carried *jeon* of all types (pages 145 to 148) perched precariously on top of pork bulgogi (page 100).

They set upon the kitchen all at once, weaving around each other to turn on burners at the stovetop, tie on aprons, and unearth serving plates from various cabinets, all while chattering to one another in Korean. I looked at my future husband, at a loss for what to do amid the hurricane. "This isn't even half of them," Andrew told me, laughing, and left to retrieve more aunts and uncles from the apartment building parking garage.

If I wasn't already nervous about making a good impression on his many aunties and uncles, now I was both nervous and lost. I figured I'd know what to do at this party after all the large Chinese potlucks my parents had attended or hosted while I was growing up, but somehow I'd forgotten the key detail—that I wouldn't understand a word of what anyone was saying—and I definitely hadn't anticipated the practiced, swift synchrony of an army of aunties who had thrown parties, cooked *bindaetteok* (page 135), marinated bulgogi, and pan-fried dumplings together for decades. I was anxious to have them think I

was helpful! And nice! And all the things a family wants their newest addition to be. However, butting into their routine felt like I'd be disrupting a well-oiled machine, and just standing there didn't seem like it would go any better.

So, half-panicking, I did the one thing everyone everywhere hates to do: I turned to the sink, where crockery and Tupperwares were piling up, and I started doing dishes. I washed the chopsticks we were using to transfer *jeon* to serving plates; I washed the giant Glasslock container that stored the raw *galbi* now sizzling merrily on a giant electric griddle that my mother-in-law had produced from nowhere; and I washed the little baby Glasslock that had held the dipping sauce for the *jeon*. I washed their lids, the tracks for the rubber rings, and the little arms that snapped the containers shut.

I washed the plastic tubs from Foodland that had held the poke now sitting neatly in a bowl, garnished with sesame seeds and scallions, and I scrubbed their lids, too. I washed the spatulas, the scissors (which, if you have never used them for cooking, are downright genius in the kitchen), and the tongs. Andrew's aunts delivered empty plates, stripped of their plastic wrap, to my elbow and disappeared again to make more food and arrange more plates. The older aunts spoke little English (or didn't need to at a party with mostly their family), but a younger one appeared next to me after awhile, smiling.

"Want to help me cook the *mandoo*?" she asked.

Her name turned out to be Auntie Christy, and she kept up a cheerful stream of part-conversation and part-instruction that slowly made me feel more at home. (She was married to the one Ha uncle, I learned, and as the one auntie not related to the others by blood, I think she recognized my plight and took pity on me.) The other aunties chatted to me with a mixture of English, lost-to-me Korean, and smiles, which always help to fill any language gap. An uncle asked me, imperiously, if I had tried his *kimchi jjigae*, which it appeared he was known for.

And once everything was cooked, plated, and arranged on the table, we ate—mounds of poke, fried *mandoo*, fish and meat and zucchini *jeon*, crisp, burnished orange *bindaetteok,* bean sprouts tossed with *gochugaru*, pink shrimp, *japchae*, and lots, and lots, and lots of kimchi.

When the night was done, the aunties descended on the kitchen with the same swift fervor they had when they arrived. This time they invited me to join in the frenzy with more than washing dishes—pointing out the foods that went in Ziploc bags, the ones that went into containers, the one Auntie Number Three (because there were so many they went by their order in age as often as they did by their name) was taking home, the plate that belonged to Auntie Christy. It's not like that party marked "the moment I became part of the Ha family," but it was a good start—because, as it turns out, behind all parties with a delicious array of food is an assortment of dishes that need washing, and if you are at a loss for how to put your best foot forward, doing those dishes is not a bad idea.

ALMOST GRANDMA HA'S KIMCHI PANCAKES
(BINDAETTEOK)

Makes 10 to 12 small pancakes (serves 3 or 4)

Before I met my husband, the only Korean pancake I'd ever encountered was seafood *pajeon,* the expansive, landscaped pancakes that were held together more by their copious fillings—octopus and shrimp and long sections of scallions—than their batter. Little did I know that that was only half of the story when it comes to Korean pancakes. My husband's family has never put *pajeon* on their dining table. Instead, the only pancakes they eat are *bindaetteok*—made not from seafood and flour, but from kimchi and mung beans.

Ask anyone in my husband's mother's family about *bindaetteok* and they will all tell you the same thing: No one in the world can make them like Grandma Ha did. On *bindaetteok* days, my husband's grandmother, parked at the griddle with a huge bowl of craggy batter, churned out pancake after pancake for her family. She served her *bindaetteok* to one person at a time only, because, according to her, it was only when the pancakes were freshest that they were most delicious. From oldest to youngest, with Grandpa Ha first down to the youngest grandchild, his family waited in line to devour hot, crispy kimchi pancakes, the next person eating only when the previous one had had his or her share. His grandmother's *bindaetteok* were unrivalled: Orange-hued from the kimchi, nutty from the mung beans, beautifully crisp on the outside, and by turns tender and crunchy inside, they were spicy and flavorful, the stuff of legends.

None of my husband's five aunties nor his mother have ever been able to replicate Grandma Ha's *bindaetteok,* even though they all make the recipe the exact same way they recall that she did. His mother surmises that it might have been the oil she fried them in (lard, perhaps?), or the skillet. Everyone at one point or another has wondered whether it had to do with the tantalizing wait. (Except my husband, who staunchly rejects that theory.) But no matter what, the *bindaetteok* are never as crisp as when she made them, nor as flavorful.

I can't claim to have done what six Ha sisters could not, but this recipe, after years of my own trials, is the closest I've come to replicating what Andrew has so fondly described. To make them as crisp and crunchy on the outside as possible, I use a cast-iron skillet, the Southern secret to perfect

1 cup dried, peeled mung beans

⅓ cup kimchi liquid or reserved starchy water from the mung beans

1½ cups well-fermented kimchi, finely chopped

1 teaspoon gochugaru

½ to 1 teaspoon salt

½ cup vegetable oil or other neutral oil, or as needed for frying

2 to 3 jalapeño or other hot chili peppers, thinly sliced (optional)

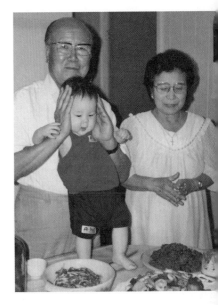

(recipe continues)

pancakes. I've also upped the amount of kimchi to more than any recipe I've ever come across, and use the leftover kimchi juice at the bottom of the jar for extra flavor. Just in case the kimchi isn't enough, I add a healthy dash of *gochugaru* for just a bit more smoky, spicy oomph. They aren't Grandma Ha's, but they are pretty darn good—so good that they were the first spicy thing our son, the youngest Ha, ever demanded more of. We like to think she would be delighted that her great-grandson, though she never got to meet him, loves them.

---

1 *The night before, or at least 6 hours in advance:* Place the mung beans in a large bowl with plenty of cold water, enough to submerge them by several inches (I use about 4 to 5 cups). Soak in the refrigerator for at least 6 hours, or overnight.

2 *The day of:* Drain the mung beans, reserving the starchy water. Place in a blender with ⅓ cup kimchi liquid, or, if you don't have any, the reserved mung bean water. Blend until the mixture forms a thick purée, about 1 minute. The mixture should be somewhat coarse but should not contain any whole mung beans, about the consistency of a very thick pancake batter.

3 In a large bowl, stir together the mung bean mixture, kimchi, gochugaru, and salt until well incorporated. You may want to reserve some of the salt and gochugaru until you've made 1 pancake and tasted it, and then adjust the taste accordingly.

4 In a 10- or 12-inch cast-iron skillet, heat 2 to 3 tablespoons oil over medium until shimmering and a drop of water sizzles when it hits the pan. Using a measuring cup, drop 2 to 3 tablespoons of batter into the pan and use the measuring cup to nudge it into a rough circle. (The batter should be thick enough that it does not spread on its own. If it does, pour the batter into a fine-mesh colander and drain off a few tablespoons of liquid.) Let the pancake sizzle merrily until the bottom reaches a deep, crispy brown, 2 to 3 minutes. If desired, place a few slices of jalapeño or other pepper on top of the pancake—it's not traditional, but we like a little extra heat. Once the bottom is nice and crisp, flip the pancake and cook on the second side until brown and crispy, about another 2 minutes. I usually make 1 pancake on its own first, to taste it and adjust seasonings, then make about 3 pancakes in the pan at once. Repeat, wiping out the skillet and adding more oil as needed, with the remaining batter. Serve immediately.

SLOW-SIMMERED SOY & BLACK PEPPER BEEF

(JANGJORIM)

Serves 6 to 8

Salty, sweet, and deeply flavorful, *jangjorim* is traditionally meant to be eaten as a small side dish or packed into lunchboxes (*dosirak*) for children, but my husband's family loved it so much when he was growing up that they enjoyed it more like a main, and now so do we. This recipe, which comes from his mother, simmers chunks of lean beef, roughly chopped onion, and whole cloves of garlic in generous glugs of soy sauce until the onions practically melt and the beef becomes so tender that it shreds with a fork. The onions and sugar combine for a demure sweetness, while the garlic adds a pungent umami. My mother-in-law throws in an abundance of Korean peppers (*gochu*) and a hearty shake of black pepper, which you don't always see in *jangjorim,* but they lace the stew with such pronounced warmth that I can't imagine it without them. And, like Red-Cooked Pork (page 149), the stew is finished off with a gaggle of hard-boiled eggs to soak up all that rich flavor. We like to make a big pot of this for a crowd, but if it's just for us, we make it on Sundays and enjoy it through the week, with kimchi, rice, and a good vegetable side—it's that kind of quick weeknight dinner that only gets better as you get closer to Friday.

---

1 Place the beef in a 4- or 5-quart Dutch oven or stockpot with the onion, Korean peppers, garlic, soy sauce, brown sugar (or honey), pepper, and enough water to fully submerge the meat (for me, usually about 3 to 4 cups). Bring the mixture just to a simmer over medium-high, then lower the heat to low and cook for about 1 hour at a very gentle simmer.

2 After 1 hour of cooking, taste the broth and adjust seasonings as needed. If you'd like more heat, add the sliced jalapeños and other seasonings as needed. (It should be quite salty.) Continue to simmer for another hour.

(recipe continues)

2 pounds flank steak, brisket, or other lean steak, sliced against the grain into cubes

1 large onion, sliced

3 to 4 Korean green chili peppers (about 3 ounces), stems trimmed (see Notes)

⅓ to ½ cup garlic cloves, peeled and smashed (about 6 to 8 cloves)

¾ to 1 cup soy sauce, or more to taste

4 to 5 tablespoons dark brown sugar, or 3 to 4 tablespoons honey

1 to 2 teaspoons black pepper

3 to 4 cups water, or as needed to cover the beef

1 to 2 jalapeño peppers, sliced in half lengthwise (if you like heat)

8 hard-boiled eggs (any size), peeled (optional)

3 If desired, add the hard-boiled eggs to the broth, making sure to submerge them as much as possible. Simmer until the meat is very tender and falls apart when a fork is inserted, and the eggs are browned, an additional hour or so. Remove from the heat, and serve hot or at room temperature. Leftovers taste even better the next day.

NOTES

Korean *gochu* peppers are generally mild. If you can't find them, *shishito* peppers also work well. For more heat, add the jalapeños at the beginning.

Some recipes call for either soaking the beef in cold water beforehand, or parboiling it to remove impurities. While you can certainly do this if you'd like, I have never noticed a huge difference in taste when skipping those steps. Instead, I just find that the gentler and the longer this stew cooks, the better—low and slow makes for the tenderest beef.

CHINESE "RUSSIAN" SOUP
(LUO SONG TANG)

Serves 4 to 6

For most of my life, I thought that my mother's *luo song tang*, or "Russian soup," was entirely her creation—a comforting, crimson bowl of hearty stew that was my mother's own quirky interpretation of what she thought Russians ate. It wasn't until I began to write this cookbook that it occurred to me to search for the meaning of *luo song tang*. To my utter surprise, it was, as you might say, a thing. In some Asian families it appears to go by "Chinese borscht," in others, "ABC soup," but whatever the moniker, it's usually uncannily similar to the bowls of savory, nourishing soup I grew up eating. There are chunks of rich beef or oxtail simmered until tender, with onions and carrots for sweetness, tomatoes for brightness, and cabbage and potatoes for heft, all in a thick, flavorful broth.

If you're unfamiliar with oxtail or can't find it, skip it and use a few pounds of some other bone-in beef that has a little bit of fat for richness. When I can find oxtail, it's generally sold sliced into round segments—these can be an adventure to pick apart, but the work makes enjoying them all the more satisfying.

---

1 Place the oxtails in a 5- to 6-quart heavy-bottomed pot or Dutch oven and cover with cold water. Bring to a boil over high heat and let bubble for about 10 minutes. Skim off any scum that rises. Meanwhile, season the steak generously with about ½ teaspoon salt and ¼ teaspoon pepper. When the oxtails have boiled for 10 minutes, drain, rinse, and set them aside.

2 Wipe out the pot and return it to medium-high heat. Add the oil and heat until shimmering. Add the onions, celery (if using), garlic, and ginger, and season generously with ½ teaspoon salt and ¼ teaspoon pepper. Cook until the vegetables begin to soften, 4 to 5 minutes. Stir in the tomato paste and cook until the paste darkens just slightly, 1 to 2 minutes.

3 Add the water, rice wine, tomatoes, carrots, oxtails, and steak to the pot. Reduce the heat to medium-low. Cover and let simmer very gently for at least 2 to 3 hours. Skim any scum or fat off the top of the soup as it forms.

(recipe continues)

2 pounds beef oxtail, trimmed of as much fat as possible

1 pound flank steak, brisket, or eye of round, sliced against the grain into cubes

1 to 2 teaspoons salt, divided

½ to 1 teaspoon black pepper, divided

1 tablespoon vegetable oil or other neutral oil

2 cups diced onion (1 to 2 onions)

½ cup diced celery (1 to 2 stalks; optional)

1 tablespoon minced garlic (2 to 3 cloves)

1 teaspoon finely grated ginger root

2 tablespoons tomato paste (or 2 to 3 tablespoons ketchup, if you don't mind a sweeter soup)

8 cups water or chicken stock

3 to 4 tablespoons Shaoxing rice wine, dry sherry, or sake

2 cups diced tomatoes (about 2 tomatoes)

1 cup diced carrots (1 to 2 carrots)

1 to 2 tablespoons dark brown sugar (optional)

4 cups diced cabbage (¼ to ½ head)

1 pound baby red potatoes, scrubbed and halved (or quartered, if large)

4 Taste the soup and adjust with more salt and pepper as needed, as well as brown sugar, if desired. Add the cabbage and potatoes, cover again, and let simmer, until the beef and potatoes are fork-tender and the cabbage is cooked through, another 20 to 30 minutes. Serve hot.

NOTES

I like to make this a day or so in advance of serving, as the flavor only improves with time, plus you can remove any fat from the top of the soup after it chills, which makes for a lighter, cleaner-tasting dish. When preparing it ahead, add the cabbage and potatoes and immediately remove from the heat. Once cool, refrigerate overnight. Before reheating, remove any solidified fat from the top of the soup, then place the pot over medium heat. Bring to a boil and then simmer for 6 to 8 minutes to cook the potatoes and cabbage to the right tenderness.

If you like firmer carrots, add them at the same time as the potatoes and cabbage.

KOREAN FRITTERS, THREE WAYS
(JEON)

Serves 4 to 6 as an appetizer

For something as simple as a few slices of fish or vegetables fried up in flour and egg, these fritters, or *jeon,* are so much more than they seem. They're savory and substantial yet light enough to snack on, and you'll hardly find a party—at least, any party thrown by my mother-in-law or anyone in my husband's family—that doesn't include a sprawling platter of at least three types, shingled neatly together around a bowl of dipping sauce. These versions are our favorites, made from bulgogi-marinated beef, zucchini, and tender white fish.

BULGOGI JEON

1 *Up to 1 day ahead, or at least 1 hour in advance:* Combine the beef, soy sauce, brown sugar, scallions, rice wine, sesame oil, and garlic in a large bowl and massage thoroughly until each piece of beef is coated in marinade. Place in an airtight container or Ziploc bag and let marinate for at least 1 hour or up to 1 day in advance.

2 *When ready to cook:* Remove the beef slices from the marinade, letting any excess drip off, and combine in a shallow plate with the flour. Toss until evenly coated in flour. Alternatively, dip the pieces into the flour one by one.

3 In a small bowl, beat the eggs until well combined.

4 Heat a large cast-iron or nonstick skillet over medium-high. Add a tablespoon or so of oil (or use cooking spray) and swirl it until it evenly coats the pan. Working one by one, dip the slices of beef into the egg batter and place into the pan in a single layer. Cook until golden-brown on one side, 1 to 2 minutes. (I usually find that the first fritters are ready to flip by the time I'm done placing the last ones in the pan.) Flip and cook on the other side until meat is cooked through and the second side is golden-brown, an additional 1 to 2 minutes. If the jeon are browning too quickly, reduce the heat to medium or medium-low. When done, remove to a plate, wipe out the skillet if needed, and repeat until all the pieces are fried. Serve immediately, with dipping sauce on the side.

1 pound thinly sliced beef rib eye, sirloin, or brisket

¼ cup soy sauce

¼ cup packed dark brown sugar

¼ cup sliced scallions (2 to 3 scallions)

2 tablespoons Shaoxing rice wine, dry sherry, or sake

1 tablespoon sesame oil

1 tablespoon minced garlic (2 to 3 cloves)

¾ cup (94 grams) flour, or more if needed

3 large eggs

2 to 3 tablespoons vegetable oil or other neutral oil, or as needed for frying

1 batch Jeon Dipping Sauce (page 148), for serving

(recipe continues)

ZUCCHINI JEON

1 pound zucchini (about 2 large or 3 medium zucchini)

½ teaspoon salt, divided, plus more to taste

½ cup (63 grams) all-purpose flour, or more if necessary (whole-wheat flour makes a great substitute)

3 large eggs

Generous pinch black pepper (optional)

2 to 3 tablespoons vegetable oil or other neutral oil, or as needed for frying

1 batch Jeon Dipping Sauce (page 148), for serving

1 Slice the zucchini into coins between ⅛- and ¼-inch thick. Spread in a large shallow dish and sprinkle evenly with salt (I usually use about ¼ teaspoon). Let sit until the coins soften just a bit, about 15 minutes.

2 Drain any water from the zucchini that was released from the salt. Add the flour and toss until all the coins are evenly dredged. (Alternatively, you can dip the coins one by one into the flour, which ensures they're dredged more evenly, but I find just tossing them together saves time and works nearly as well.)

3 In a small bowl, beat together the eggs, ¼ teaspoon salt, and pepper (if using), until well combined.

4 Heat a large cast-iron or nonstick skillet over medium-high. Add a tablespoon or so of oil (or use cooking spray) and swirl it until it evenly coats the pan. Working one by one, dip the zucchini coins into the egg batter, then place them into the pan in a single layer. Cook until golden-brown, 1 to 2 minutes. (I usually find that the first fritters are ready to flip by the time I'm done placing the last ones in the pan.) Flip and cook until that side is also golden-brown, an additional 1 to 2 minutes. If the jeon are browning too quickly, reduce the heat to medium or medium-low. When done, remove to a plate, wipe out the skillet if needed, and repeat. (You may want to taste one as you go to check whether it's salty enough for your liking, and add more salt to the egg mixture if needed.) When all the zucchini coins are fried, serve immediately, with dipping sauce on the side.

(recipe continues)

FISH JEON

1 pound haddock, cod, or other mild white fish

½ teaspoon salt, divided

¼ teaspoon black pepper, divided (optional)

¾ cup (94 grams) flour, or more if needed

3 large eggs

¼ cup sliced scallions (2 to 3 scallions)

1 tablespoon minced garlic (2 to 3 cloves)

2 to 3 tablespoons vegetable oil or other neutral oil, or as needed for frying

1 batch Jeon Dipping Sauce (recipe follows), for serving

1 Slice the fish into thin pieces about ¼-inch thick and 2 to 3 inches wide. Season with ¼ teaspoon salt and ⅛ teaspoon pepper and let sit for 10 to 15 minutes.

2 Add the flour to the fish slices and toss gently until evenly coated. Alternatively, dip the pieces into the flour one by one.

3 In a small bowl, beat together the eggs, scallions, garlic, and remaining salt and pepper (if using) until well combined.

4 Heat a large cast-iron or nonstick skillet over medium-high. Add a tablespoon or so of oil (or use cooking spray) and swirl it until it evenly coats the pan. Working one by one, dip the fish into the egg batter and place into the pan in a single layer. Cook until golden-brown on one side, 1 to 2 minutes. (I usually find that the first fritters are ready to flip by the time I'm done placing the last ones in the pan.) Flip and cook on the other side until the fish is cooked through, flakes easily, and the second side is golden-brown, an additional 1 to 2 minutes. If the jeon are browning too quickly, reduce the heat to medium or medium-low. When done, remove to a plate, wipe out the skillet if needed, and repeat until all the fish pieces are fried. (You may want to taste one as you go to check whether it's salty enough for your liking, and add more salt to the egg mixture if needed.) Serve immediately, with dipping sauce on the side.

---

2 tablespoons soy sauce

2 tablespoons rice vinegar

1 tablespoon dark brown sugar

½ teaspoon sesame oil

½ to 1 teaspoon gochugaru (Korean chili powder), depending on preferred spice level

2 tablespoons chopped scallions

½ teaspoon toasted sesame seeds (optional)

1 to 2 tablespoons water, as needed for thinning

jeon dipping sauce

MAKES ABOUT ⅓ CUP, OR ENOUGH FOR 1 BATCH OF JEON

In a small bowl, mix together the soy sauce, vinegar, sugar, oil, gochugaru, scallions, and sesame seeds (if using). Thin with water to your desired consistency, and serve. The sauce will keep for several days in the fridge.

NOTES

If you have any left over, this makes for a good, slightly different alternative to the dipping sauce for Potstickers (page 157).

RED-COOKED PORK
(HONG SHAO ROU)

Serves 4 to 6

This classic Shanghainese dish is the first way that I ever enjoyed pork belly, with ruby-red chunks of meltingly buttery pork cloaked in a glossy sweet-salty sauce, and after all the various preparations of pork belly that have appeared on the restaurant scene, it is still—to me—the best one. The meat is quickly parboiled to remove any scum, tossed in a hot wok with sugar until caramelized and heavenly fragrant, then simmered slowly and gently in soy sauce, scallions, ginger, and star anise until it all reduces into a lustrous glaze. You can keep it simple and make the pork the star of the show, or you can toss in my favorite additions—knots made from tofu skin (*fu zhu*) and hard-boiled eggs.

---

1 Bring a large pot of water to a boil over medium-high heat. Add the pork and boil for about 10 minutes, skimming off any scum as it forms on top of the water. Drain the pork and rinse to remove any remaining scum, then set aside.

2 In a large wok, combine the sugar and 2 tablespoons water over medium-high heat and stir until just dissolved. Swirl the mixture without stirring just until it bubbles and begins to turn slightly darker in certain spots, 3 to 4 minutes. Add the cubed pork belly to the wok and sauté it with the caramelized sugar until pork is browned and smells fragrant, 3 to 4 more minutes.

3 Add the scallions, garlic, ginger, and star anise and toss for 1 to 2 minutes to give the aromatics a quick cook. Add the rice wine, both soy sauces, and enough water to cover the pork, about 3 to 4 cups. Stir to combine, then cover and simmer over low heat until the pork is tender, at least 1 hour, or you can keep it at a low simmer for even longer, 2 hours or more, if you'd like it even tenderer.

4 Once the pork is tender, uncover and turn the heat back to medium-high. Simmer until the sauce reduces to a smooth consistency, another 10 to 15 minutes. Taste and adjust with more soy sauce or sugar, if desired. Enjoy hot, over rice. Leftovers will only improve with time, and can be frozen and reheated wonderfully.

(recipe continues)

2 pounds pork belly or pork shoulder (I prefer a leaner pork belly, if you can find it, or a combination of belly and shoulder), cubed

¼ cup sugar, plus more to taste

3 to 4 scallions, cut into 2-inch pieces (about ¼ cup sliced)

3 to 4 garlic cloves, smashed, or 1 tablespoon minced garlic

1 inch ginger root, sliced into 6 to 8 pieces

3 whole star anise

⅓ cup Shaoxing rice wine, dry sherry, or sake

3 tablespoons light (regular) soy sauce, plus more to taste

3 to 4 teaspoons dark soy sauce (see Notes)

Cooked rice, for serving

NOTES

If you can track it down at a Chinese supermarket or find it on Amazon, dark soy sauce helps create the glossy, viscous red sauce that gives rise to the name of this dish. If you don't have it, don't worry—I generally find that it does more for the appearance of the dish than the flavor, and have always loved this every bit as much when made with only light soy sauce. If you like, though, you can add a teaspoon or two of molasses to compensate.

Some recipes call for blanching the pork belly in long strips (as it is often sold) and cubing it only after blanching. This can help preserve the shape of the pork belly after cooking. For ease, and so that I don't have to wait for the meat to cool between steps, I prefer to cube it raw. But you should feel free to experiment with both methods.

If you like, you can add a few extra goodies to this dish during the last 20 to 30 minutes of cooking. *Dried bean-curd (tofu) knots or sticks* made from tofu skin are my very favorite addition for their chewy texture and ability to soak up the flavor of the sauce—I end up picking out every last one when I include them. That said, they can be hard to find without forking over a markup cost on Amazon or trekking to a specialty supermarket. If you do find them, soak about 2 to 3 cups' worth for 6 to 8 hours, or overnight, before adding them during the last 20 minutes of cooking. You may need to add a bit more water and soy sauce to compensate. *Hard-boiled eggs* are also a welcome addition for many of the same reasons (and they pop up in the same role in *jangjorim,* page 139). If you decide to use them, make a few slits lengthwise in the eggs before adding them to better soak up the flavor. You can use anywhere from 4 to 6 eggs, and add them during the last 30 minutes of cooking.

Note that these additions soak up sauce and will make it less likely to turn glossy and thick—but are so tasty that it's worth it!

MY GREAT-GRANDMOTHER'S LION'S HEAD MEATBALLS
(SHI ZI TOU)

Serves 4

FOR THE BOK CHOY

1½ pounds bok choy (Shanghai baby bok choy is my favorite, but larger varieties will work, too)

1 tablespoon soy sauce

½ tablespoon sesame oil

¼ teaspoon salt

FOR THE MEATBALLS

1 pound ground pork

¼ cup finely sliced scallions (2 to 3 scallions)

1 teaspoon finely grated ginger root

1 tablespoon minced garlic (2 to 3 cloves)

3 tablespoons sugar

3 tablespoons soy sauce

1 tablespoon Shaoxing rice wine, dry sherry, or sake

1 tablespoon sesame oil

1 teaspoon salt

3 large eggs

¼ cup cornstarch

1 cup vegetable oil or other neutral oil, or as needed for frying

Cooked rice, for serving

My father's earliest memories of Shanghainese food come from his grandmother, who raised him for most of his childhood. She made him savory Shanghainese fava beans, or *can dou*, flash-fried in a wok until tender; large, puffy steamed buns (page 64) when they could get their hands on good flour; wontons in soup (page 166); and regal Shanghainese lion's head meatballs. She churned out these dishes in the narrow kitchen of her stately old townhouse in a network of alleys in Shanghai, carrying them up the stairs from the kitchen into the front room where they'd eat, and she cooked them for him whenever he visited all the way until my father grew up, moved to the States, and came back with me in tow.

Oil was hard to come by back then, and used only sparingly, but my dad remembers these meatballs being a worthy cause for a splurge. The meatballs are shallow-fried in just enough oil to give each side that brown, Maillard umami, then tucked into an impossibly tall pile of bok choy, where it's all steamed until the meatballs are soft, tender, and rich, and the bok choy wilts into a savory-sweet heap under the oil and juices. They turn out comfortingly flavorful without being overwhelming—a true homestyle food, the kind that feels like your grandmother's hug, and lingers with you like a good memory should.

1 *Prep the bok choy:* Thoroughly wash and clean the bok choy, aiming to leave the heads more or less intact, except for trimming the very ends of the stems. (This method is best for small, Shanghai baby bok choy. If you are using larger, tougher bok choy, feel free to separate the leaves.) Place the bok choy in a heavy-bottomed 4-quart pot. It should more or less fill the pot to the top, which will look like too much, but it will be just right once the bok choy steams and wilts. It will amaze you how much they shrink. Drizzle the bok choy with soy sauce and sesame oil, and sprinkle with salt. Set the pot aside.

2 *For the meatballs:* In a large bowl, combine the ground pork, scallions, ginger, garlic, sugar, soy sauce, rice wine, sesame oil, and salt, and stir with chopsticks or a wooden spoon until well blended. Next, add the eggs and mix vigorously until well combined. The mixture will

seem loose and liquidy; this is okay. Add the cornstarch and mix again until the mixture forms a porridge-like consistency, like a thick muffin batter.

3 Pour the vegetable oil into a large wok or nonstick skillet, enough to coat the bottom with about ½ inch of oil. Turn the heat to medium-high and give the oil a few minutes to heat up. When the oil reaches 375°F to 400°F, or a wooden chopstick bubbles energetically when inserted into the oil, use a ¼-cup measuring cup or large ice cream scoop to drop balls of the pork mixture into the wok in a single layer. (I fry 4 or 5 balls at a time, and end up frying in 2 or 3 batches.) Let them sizzle in the pan until nicely browned, 2 to 3 minutes, then flip and brown the other side, another 3 minutes or so. They do not need to cook through, since they'll be finished in the steamer. Once the meatballs are browned on both sides, transfer them with a slotted spoon to set on top of the pre-pared bok choy. Repeat with the remaining pork mixture.

4 Once all the meatballs are browned and nestled on top of the bok choy, cover the pot and place over medium-low heat. Let the bok choy and meatballs steam until the meatballs are cooked through and the bok choy leaves have wilted and the stems are tender, 20 to 30 minutes. Remove from the heat. Serve warm, with plenty of rice.

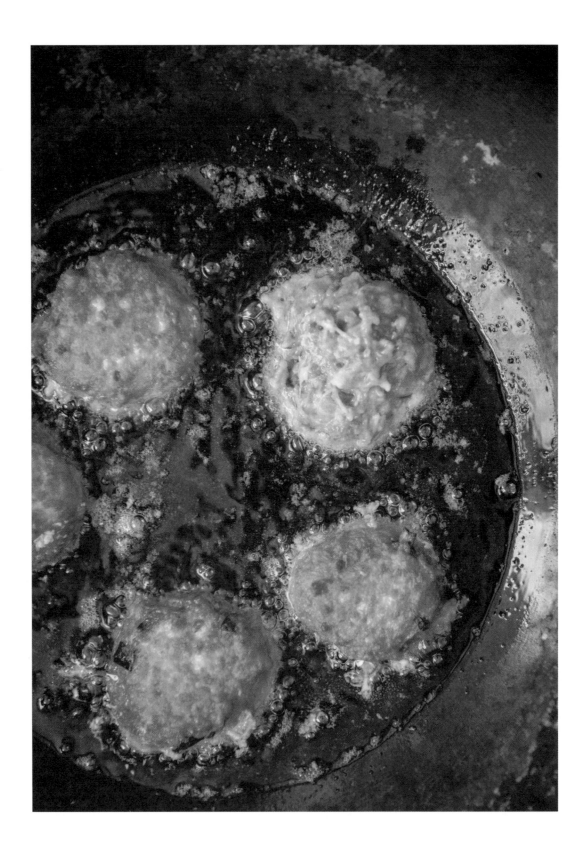

POTSTICKERS
(GUO TIE)

Makes 24 to 32 dumplings (serves 2 or 3)

To me, there's hardly anything more satisfying than devouring my way through a platter of homemade potstickers. I can still remember the first time I ever had one—*guo tie* in Chinese, translated literally as "potstick"—in a Shanghai breakfast house as a child. My household tended toward boiled dumplings, so my first experience crunching into a fried potsticker, stuffed with a juicy pork filling and irresistibly crisp on the bottom, was love at first bite.

Though a tad time-consuming, potstickers are gloriously easy to make at home. The dough for the wrappers is elegant simplicity at its best, the very same dough used in Ginger-Scallion Chicken & Dumplings (page 79) and kimchi *sujebi* (page 82), and my favorite pork filling is hearty and savory, with just a bit of crunch from plenty of vegetables. I now like to roll my wrappers a bit thicker than my Southern Chinese parents prefer, after becoming smitten with the "Peking ravioli" widely offered at Chinese restaurants in Boston. True to their Bostonian nicknames, potstickers in Beijing and the northern parts of China are chewier and doughier than the norm. If you're partial to a more delicate dumpling, however, feel free to use store-bought gyoza wrappers, or just roll the dough out to a thinner, more pasta-like thickness.

---

1 If using regular cabbage or another leafy vegetable, skip this step. If using napa cabbage, rinse the cabbage, then sprinkle ¼ teaspoon salt over the leaves and let it sit until it wilts and releases water, 10 to 15 minutes. (Otherwise, the water is released while cooking and can result in soggy dumplings.)

2 Combine the cabbage and pork together in a large bowl. Add ½ teaspoon salt, the scallions, soy sauce, sesame oil, rice wine, garlic, ginger, and sugar, and mix well. Sprinkle the cornstarch evenly over the mixture and mix again until well combined. Cover and chill in the refrigerator while you roll out the dumpling wrappers.

(recipe continues)

FOR THE FILLING

1½ cups shredded napa cabbage, or 1 cup shredded regular cabbage (see step 1), or 1 cup other hardy, leafy vegetable (kale, Swiss chard, or even shaved Brussels sprouts work well here)

½ teaspoon salt, plus ¼ teaspoon more if using napa cabbage

½ pound ground pork (ground chicken or turkey also work well here)

¼ cup finely sliced scallions (2 to 3 scallions)

2 tablespoons soy sauce

2 teaspoons sesame oil

1 tablespoon Shaoxing rice wine, dry sherry, or sake

2 teaspoons minced garlic (1 to 2 cloves)

1 teaspoon finely grated ginger root

½ to 1 tablespoon sugar, to taste

1 tablespoon cornstarch

TO ASSEMBLE AND FRY

1 batch Dumpling Dough (page 78)

All-purpose flour, for rolling

1 to 2 tablespoons neutral oil

(ingredients continue)

2 tablespoons Chinkiang
black vinegar

2 tablespoons soy sauce

2 to 3 teaspoons chili garlic
paste (1 to 2 teaspoons
sriracha also works)

1 teaspoon dark
brown sugar

3 *To roll the wrappers the traditional way:* Divide the dough into 4 equal balls. Working with 1 ball at a time and keeping the others covered or in a sealed container, roll the dough out into a short cylinder. Cut into about 6 to 8 pieces—fewer for thicker skins and more for thinner ones. Use a small Chinese rolling pin or other small dowel to roll each piece of dough into a circle about 3½ to 4 inches in diameter, aiming to make the edges a bit thinner than the center. Flour generously and set aside, covered. Repeat with the rest of the dough.

4 *To roll the wrappers using a biscuit cutter:* Divide the dough into 4 equal balls. Working with 1 ball at a time and keeping the others covered or in a sealed container, roll the ball at least ⅛-inch thick, preferably a bit thinner. Using a 3½- to 4-inch biscuit or cookie cutter, cut as many rounds as you can from the dough (I aim for at least 4). Flour the wrappers generously and set aside, covered. Reroll the scraps as needed. If the scraps begin to resist your rolling pin, place them back into the container with the remaining dough until they soften again. Repeat with the rest of the dough. I usually get about 24 wrappers if aiming for a thicker skin, and up to 32 if aiming for a thinner one.

5 *To pleat:* To pleat the dumplings, place 2 to 3 teaspoons of filling in the center of a wrapper. Lightly fold the wrapper in half to make a half-moon shape, like you're making a taco, but keep the edges apart. Dampen the inside of one edge to help seal, if needed, then gently make pleats, pressing one side to the other as you go. Once the dumpling is fully pleated, pinch all along the pleats to make sure the dumpling is tightly sealed. Place the dumpling on a plate, seam-side up, and press down slightly to create a flat bottom. Set aside and cover with a damp dish towel while you pleat the rest. Alternatively, simply place 2 to 3 teaspoons of filling in the center of 1 wrapper, then fold in half and pinch the edges shut to form a flat half-moon.

6 *To cook:* In a large skillet or wok that can be covered, heat about 1 tablespoon oil over medium-high until shimmering. Add as many dumplings as will fit in a ring around the edge of the pan, flat-side down. If you like, you can leave a little room in between to ensure they won't stick to one another.

(recipe continues)

7 Cook the dumplings until the bottoms are crisp and nicely browned, about 2 minutes. Drizzle 2 to 4 tablespoons of water into the pan (enough to cover the bottom of the pan) and cover. Steam until the dumplings are cooked through and the wrappers are no longer doughy, 4 to 6 minutes. If the water cooks off during that time, add another tablespoon or so, and reduce the heat to medium.

8 *Meanwhile, make the dipping sauce:* Mix all the sauce ingredients together. Set aside until ready to eat.

9 *To finish:* When the dumplings are cooked through, remove the cover and let any residual liquid in the pan cook off—this helps nice crisp crusts form on the bottoms of the dumplings. Remove to a plate, wipe out the skillet or wok, and repeat as necessary with the remaining dumplings. Serve immediately, with dipping sauce on the side.

NOTES

To boil your dumplings: If you prefer, you can boil your dumplings instead of frying them into potstickers. Bring a large pot of water to a boil and add as many dumplings as can comfortably fit in a single layer in the pot. Let cook until the dumplings float, about 3 minutes. Let boil another 1 to 2 minutes, until cooked through, then use a slotted spoon to transfer them to a plate. Repeat with any remaining dumplings. Serve immediately, with dipping sauce on the side.

SHANGHAI-STYLE SWEET & SOUR BABY-BACK RIBS

Serves 3 to 4

When it comes to food, my father is a creature of habit. While my mother urges us to try the newest falafel place in town or comes home gushing about her first taste of chicken tikka masala, my dad gravitates toward the familiar, looking for the comforting Chinese food of his childhood wherever he goes.

There are a few exceptions—my father is a surprising but ardent supporter of Pizza Hut—but for the most part, my dad's thirty years in the United States hasn't changed his tastes. He hopefully suggests going to a Chinese restaurant whenever we decide to eat out as a family, whether we're in California or South Carolina or on a vacation in Germany, and if we don't go to a Chinese restaurant, he divines a dish from the menu that is closest to what he knows.

At barbecue restaurants in my hometown in South Carolina, my father's favorite dish became baby-back ribs, smoked until tender and slathered with a sweet-and-sour barbecue sauce. I never considered why that might be until we went to Shanghai a few years back and enjoyed Shanghainese short ribs for an appetizer. Just like the American South, the Chinese "South" prepares their ribs with a sticky glaze that uses vinegar as one main ingredient and sugar as another—it's simply Chinkiang black vinegar instead, with a few other flavors, like soy and sesame, in the mix, slathered on short, chopped ribs instead of long racks of baby-back ribs. This version combines American-style baby-back ribs, prepared in an oven (which is deceptively and unexpectedly easy), with a Shanghai-style sweet-and-sour glaze, for a dish that might just be familiar to both cultures.

3 pounds pork baby-back ribs

½ cup plus 2 tablespoons packed dark brown sugar

½ cup Chinkiang black vinegar (balsamic vinegar works in a pinch)

¼ cup soy sauce

¼ cup Shaoxing rice wine, dry sherry, or sake

¼ cup sliced scallions (2 to 3 scallions), plus more for garnish (optional)

1 inch ginger root, sliced into 6 pieces

1 tablespoon minced garlic (2 to 3 cloves)

¼ teaspoon white pepper

½ tablespoon toasted sesame seeds, to garnish (optional)

---

1 Preheat the oven to 275°F. Place a piece of foil, large enough to fold and seal around the ribs, on a rimmed baking sheet. Place the rack of ribs meat-side down on the foil and prick the membrane several times.

2 In a medium bowl, mix together ½ cup brown sugar, the vinegar, soy sauce, rice wine, scallions, ginger, garlic, and white pepper. Pour half the marinade over the ribs, lifting them to allow the marinade to pool underneath, and fold the foil up around the ribs, sealing tightly. Reserve the other half of the marinade for basting.

(recipe continues)

3 Transfer the foil packet to a sheet pan and bake for about 2 to 3 hours, until a fork slides easily through the meat and the meat has pulled away from the bone. If you find your fork is encountering resistance, continue baking for an additional 30 minutes or more, until the meat is tender. Remove from the oven and let cool, still wrapped, for about 15 minutes.

4 Increase the oven temperature to 350°F. Open the foil and carefully drain the juices, reserving about ¼ cup. Pour the ¼ cup of juice into a small saucepan and add the reserved marinade. Bring to a simmer over medium-high heat and cook, stirring regularly, until the marinade thickens and coats the back of a spoon, 6 to 7 minutes.

5 Position the ribs meat-side up and brush them with marinade. Return to the oven, leaving the foil open, and bake, basting the ribs with more marinade every 10 minutes, until the meat is very tender, a total of 50 to 60 more minutes.

6 During the last 10 minutes of baking, use any leftover marinade to make a dipping sauce. Return the marinade to the stove and add the remaining 2 tablespoons brown sugar. Cook over medium-low heat, stirring occasionally, until the sauce thickens and turns viscous, 2 to 3 minutes. Remove from the heat and set aside.

7 When the meat is done, remove from the oven and cut the rack into individual rib segments. Garnish with sesame seeds and more scallions, if desired, and serve immediately, with the sauce on the side for dipping.

NOTES

If you find the ribs aren't coming out as tender as you'd like, reduce the heat to 225°F in the first step and bake for longer, about 4 hours, before moving on to basting and baking for an additional 50 to 60 minutes. Also, I have found that when doubling the batch and baking more ribs at once, I have needed to increase the baking time.

SPICY BRAISED LAMB WITH RADISHES & NOODLES

Serves 6 to 8

2 pounds lamb shank
(about 2 shanks)

2 cups radishes (about
20 bulbs), with the greens
on top intact

2 tablespoons vegetable oil
or other neutral oil

4 scallions, sliced into
2-inch pieces (about
½ cup sliced)

⅓ cup garlic cloves, peeled
and smashed (5 to 6 cloves)

1 inch ginger root, sliced
into 6 to 8 pieces

5- to 6-inch sprig
rosemary

1 cup Shaoxing rice wine,
dry sherry, or sake

⅓ cup soy sauce, or more
to taste

2 tablespoons dark
brown sugar

3 to 4 tablespoons
chili garlic paste
(1 to 2 tablespoons
sriracha also works)

FOR SERVING

2 pounds fresh Chinese
noodles, dried wide broad
bean noodles, cellophane
noodles, or other noodles
of your choice (most long
pastas work just fine here)

¼ cup cilantro or parsley
leaves, chopped

I've never come across lamb shank made this way anywhere but in my mother's kitchen—and I've never had lamb *this good* anywhere else, either. The shanks are braised in layers of complex flavors, gradually added one by one by my mother over the years as she experimented with lamb's strong, distinctive taste. The radishes, pink and cheerful, add a welcome brightness to the soup and help cut any gamey flavor from the meat, as does the sprig of rosemary. As the lamb shanks cook down into tender, fall-apart chunks, the chili garlic paste adds heat and the soy sauce laces the soup with umami. Cilantro (or parsley, if you prefer) finishes the soup with a little extra zing, and noodles cooked during the last few minutes soak up all the nuanced flavors into hearty, slurpable bites. My mother knows this dish is my favorite; it's the one she always has cooking on the stove when I come home for visits.

---

1 Preheat the oven to 300°F. In a large ovenproof pot (see Notes), bring 4 quarts of water to a boil over medium-high heat. Add the lamb shanks and cook for 5 to 10 minutes, skimming off any scum that forms. Meanwhile, cut the radishes from their tops, reserving the greens, and trim the ends. Set both the greens and the radishes aside (discard the ends).

2 Drain the shanks and rinse them to remove any remaining scum. Dry the pot and place it back over medium-high heat. Add the oil. Once the oil is shimmering, add the scallions, garlic, ginger, and rosemary, and cook until the aromatics just begin to turn fragrant, 2 to 3 minutes.

3 Add the lamb shanks, trimmed radishes, rice wine, soy sauce, brown sugar, and chili garlic paste, along with enough water to cover the shanks (I usually add about 5 to 6 cups). Give the mixture a few stirs to incorporate, then bring it to a simmer. Cover the pot and place it in the oven.

4 Cook for about 2 hours, turning the lamb shanks and adding more water every 45 minutes or so if the liquids have cooked off. After 2 hours, remove from the oven and add the radish greens. Set the pot on the stove over medium-low heat and simmer until the shanks shred easily and both the radishes and their greens are very tender, 30 to 45 minutes. Meanwhile, cook the noodles of your choice according to the package directions.

5 When the lamb is done, pull the meat from the bones and discard the bones. Add the meat back to the pot, along with the cilantro, and give it a stir. Taste and adjust seasonings if needed. To serve, divide the noodles, meat, radishes, and radish greens among 6 to 8 bowls. Alternatively, stir the noodles right into the pot and let your guests serve themselves.

NOTES

If you don't have an ovenproof pot, simply cook the shanks on the stovetop on a low simmer for about 2 hours, before adding the radish greens and proceeding with step 4. The heat will be a bit less even, but you'll end up with a dish that's just as tasty.

COLLARD WONTONS

Yields 70 to 80 wontons, or enough for 4 to 6

FOR THE WONTONS

½ pound collard greens, roughly chopped

1 pound ground pork

¼ cup thinly sliced scallions (2 to 3 scallions)

1 tablespoon finely grated ginger root

3 tablespoons Shaoxing rice wine, dry sherry, or sake

2 tablespoons sesame oil

2 tablespoons soy sauce

1 tablespoon sugar (optional)

½ teaspoon salt

¼ teaspoon white pepper

70 to 80 wonton wrappers (15 to 16 ounces, or about 1⅓ packages; keep unused wrappers covered in plastic wrap, sealed in a Ziploc bag, and frozen for later use)

FOR THE BROTH

4 cups water

4 cups chicken broth

1 to 2 teaspoons soy sauce, for serving

½ teaspoon sesame oil, for serving

¼ cup thinly sliced scallions (2 to 3 scallions), for serving

In our house, making wontons began late in the afternoon. My mother started it off by making the filling—squeezing the moisture from greens, chopping them with her heavy, Chinese-style cleaver, and stirring them together with ground pork, garlic, ginger, and various fragrant condiments. Next, the bowl landed on our kitchen table, where my father waited, cross-legged. Peeling the wonton wrappers off a block, he laid neat dollops of filling on them one by one, then tossed them flat on the table in front of him. Once he'd amassed a long row he'd pick them up and fold them into plump little bundles before lining them up in neat spirals on platters that were returned to my mother to be simmered in broth.

When I think back on wonton nights, I hear the light pitter-patter of wonton wrappers hitting the table and see my dad's impossibly quick, origami-like folding, producing beautifully uniform wontons with their little chests puffed up proud and boisterous, as though they knew how well they were made. When my parents had Shanghainese friends over, they'd join the process as though they'd been there the entire time, filling and folding the wontons seamlessly the way my dad always had—I was startled the first time I saw it, surprised that anyone else knew what I'd thought were our own wonton family secrets, but food, as I've learned over and over, is a language you don't need to grow up speaking together to understand.

My mother typically uses a pungent, fragrant Chinese vegetable called shepherd's purse, or *ji cai*, but since this is hard to come by even in some Asian supermarkets, I've swapped in an unlikely but worthy substitute native to my childhood home—collard greens. Surprisingly, collards add just the right bite to the wontons, mimicking the slight spicy kick of shepherd's purse so closely that I might not know the difference if I hadn't made it myself. If you can't find either of these, though, any hardy leafy green will do (kale, Swiss chard, or cabbage all work).

1 Bring a large pot of water to a boil over high heat. Add the greens and reduce the heat to medium. Simmer until the greens are bright green and beginning to turn tender, but still have some bite, 10 to 15 minutes. Drain and add to a food processor. Pulse until finely shredded.

2 In a large bowl, combine the greens, pork, scallions, ginger, rice wine, sesame oil, soy sauce, sugar (if using), salt, and white pepper. Using chopsticks or a wooden spoon, stir vigorously until all ingredients are well combined and the filling forms a thick paste.

3 Prepare a small bowl of water for sealing the wrappers. For each wrapper, place 1 teaspoon of filling in the center. Dab a bit of water on one edge and fold the wrapper in half, taking care to seal the wrapper well around the filling. Dab water on one corner of the folded seam and bring the two folded corners together to form a small bundle (see page 168). Place on a tray and repeat. You should end up with 70 to 80 wontons. To save them for later, freeze on the tray, then place in a Ziploc bag. They'll keep in the freezer for up to 6 months.

4 When you're ready to cook the wontons, in a large pot, bring the water and chicken broth to a boil. Add about 20 wontons, stirring gently to ensure they don't stick to the bottom of the pot. Cook until the water comes back to a boil and the wontons float to the surface, about 2 minutes. Using a slotted spoon, transfer the wontons to plate. Repeat with the remaining wontons until they're all cooked, or freeze a portion of the uncooked wontons for later. To cook from frozen, use the same method, but boil for 4 to 6 minutes, until the wontons float.

5 To serve, divide the wontons among several small bowls and ladle a bit of the cooking broth over each bowl. Drizzle lightly with soy sauce and a few drops of sesame oil, and top with scallions. Enjoy immediately.

A GOOD MAKE-AHEAD CHILI

Serves 8

1 tablespoon olive oil

2 cups diced or minced
onion (about 1 large onion)

2 tablespoons minced
garlic (5 to 6 cloves)

Salt and black pepper,
to taste

1 cup diced or minced
carrots (4 to 5 carrots)

1 cup diced or minced
celery (about 2 stalks)

½ cup diced bell pepper
(about 1 bell pepper)

2 pounds ground beef
(preferably 86% lean or
more)

3 to 4 tablespoons chili
powder

2 teaspoons cumin

½ teaspoon paprika

¼ to ½ teaspoon crushed
red pepper flakes,
or more to taste

¼ teaspoon cayenne
pepper, or more to taste

1 (28-ounce) can crushed
tomatoes

1 (14-ounce) can diced
tomatoes

1 (14-ounce) can black
beans, drained and rinsed

1 jalapeño pepper, seeded
and sliced (or seeds left in,
for more heat)

It is my opinion that a good, respectable chili is a necessity in anyone's kitchen repertoire. This is ours, made the way we like it—thick and hearty, heavy on the beef but light on the beans, plenty of smoky spice and a present but not overwhelming sweetness, for a flavorful chili that only gets better as it sits in the fridge overnight. I grew up eating chili on its own or with a thick slice of cornbread (page 213), but my husband enjoys it the Hawaii way, with plenty of white rice. Both are delicious, and both are best when you don't hold back on the toppings.

1 Heat the olive oil in a large pot (at least 5 quarts) over medium until shimmering. Add the onion and garlic, season generously with salt and black pepper (I use about ¼ to ½ teaspoon salt and ¼ teaspoon pepper at each step), and sauté just until the onion begins to soften, 2 to 3 minutes. Add the carrots, celery, and bell pepper, season again with salt and black pepper, and continue to sauté until onion begins to turn translucent and the other vegetables begin to soften, another 2 to 3 minutes.

2 Add the beef and continue to cook, breaking up the beef into small pieces, until the meat is browned and no longer pink, about 5 minutes. Add the chili powder, cumin, paprika, red pepper flakes, salt, black pepper, and cayenne, and stir until well combined. You may want to start with a smaller quantity of spices and adjust to taste as the chili cooks.

3 Add the crushed and diced tomatoes, black beans, jalapeño, ketchup (if using), and brown sugar. Stir until well incorporated, then reduce the heat to low and let simmer for at least 1 hour, ideally 2 or 3. If the chili cooks down too thick, add water or chicken stock, ¼ cup or so at a time, to thin it out to your liking. When done, adjust the seasonings, and serve with plenty of white rice, sour cream, shredded cheddar, sliced scallions, diced onions, and more sliced jalapeño. As the title suggests, the chili just gets better the next day.

NOTES

If you have an ovenproof pot, such as a Dutch oven, this chili is also excellent if simmered in the oven at 350°F for 1 to 3 hours instead of on the stove, in a method similar to the lamb *ragù* (page 122) or the spicy braised lamb (page 164).

If using ketchup and brown sugar, the chili will come out on the sweeter side—you might want to hold off on the sugar for a less sweet chili.

¼ cup ketchup (optional)

2 to 3 tablespoons dark brown sugar, or more to taste

Water or chicken stock (optional, as needed to thin)

FOR SERVING

Cooked white rice (about 1 cup per person)

Sour cream

Shredded cheddar cheese

Sliced scallions

Diced raw onion

Sliced jalapeño peppers

CHINESE COLA CHICKEN WINGS

Serves 3 or 4

During my first year of law school, I shared the communal kitchen on my floor with a group of Chinese international students who loved cooking. They were kind enough to include me in their evening adventures in the kitchen, and I usually hung out in the corner, listening to them chatter while they prepared mouthwatering creations in a large wok. Some dishes were new to me and others were wonderfully familiar, like Chinese Scrambled Eggs & Tomatoes (page 195) or Tea Eggs (page 184).

One night I walked into the kitchen to find, to my amazement, a girl pouring a can of Coke over chicken wings. What could a can of soda possibly be doing in a Chinese dish? I watched, with more than a little incredulity, as the soda foamed inexplicably into a velvety, glossy sauce that was indistinguishable in appearance to the more traditional soy-glazed dishes I grew up with. This was the first surprise; the second surprise was, upon trying a wing that she offered me, how absolutely delicious it was. As it turns out, soda simmered with soy sauce and a few aromatics results in a sticky, savory-sweet soy glaze that betrays no trace of carbonated artificial flavor. Simple to prepare, yet nearly identical in flavor to dishes like Red-Cooked Pork (page 149), there's a reason these wings are popular in China. They were so good that I emailed her later, after we'd all left for the summer, for the recipe. She was kind enough to share it, and here it is.

---

1 Make 2 or 3 small cuts on each of the chicken wings to help them absorb the sauce. Place the wings in a large bowl with the rice wine, salt, and white pepper and toss to evenly coat. Let marinate in the refrigerator for 15 to 20 minutes, then drain, reserving the marinade.

2 Heat the oil in a large wok over high until shimmering. Add the chicken wings, ginger, garlic, scallions, and star anise (if using), and cook, stirring occasionally, until the wings get a bit of nice browning here and there, 3 to 4 minutes. Add the reserved marinade, cola, and soy sauce, and reduce the heat to medium. (The cola will foam up quite a bit, but will subside into a simmer.) Let simmer, turning the wings occasionally, until the sauce reduces and thickly coats the wings, about 15 minutes. Serve with rice and plenty of napkins.

2 pounds chicken wings, cut in half at the joint

¼ cup Shaoxing rice wine, dry sherry, or sake

¼ teaspoon salt

¼ teaspoon white pepper

2 tablespoons vegetable oil or other neutral oil

½ inch ginger root, sliced into 3 or 4 pieces

1 tablespoon minced garlic (2 to 3 cloves)

¼ cup sliced scallions (2 to 3 scallions)

1 star anise (optional)

1 cup cola, such as Coca-Cola or Pepsi (*do not use diet or sugar-free versions; if you prefer, you can use ¾ cup water and ¼ cup packed dark brown sugar instead*)

¼ cup soy sauce

Cooked rice, for serving

NOTES

If you don't have a wok, a 12-inch skillet will work as well, but you may get a bit less browning (especially if using a nonstick skillet) and you may want to turn the wings more frequently, to make sure all sides are submerged in the sauce.

SHANGHAINESE CUCUMBER SALAD, TWO WAYS

Serves 2 or 3 as a side

Hardly any Chinese dinner is complete without a dish of cucumber salad on the side, smashed until craggy and infused with tang, umami, and a touch of heat. Growing up, we always made our cucumber salad two ways, hot and cold. The cold version is more typical, an addictive blend of vinegar, sesame oil, soy, and just a touch of sugar and red pepper flakes—it works well, too, with peeled broccoli stems—but my mother, who has a sensitive stomach and prefers things warm, likes to flash-fry her cucumbers instead, with garlic, scallion, and sesame oil. The quick fry changes everything, making the cucumbers just a touch softer and mellowing the sesame oil with the garlic and scallions into a round, warm flavor. Even though my mother only does it to avoid a bellyache, I've come to love cucumber salad the way she makes it just as much as the alternative. Use thin-skinned Persian or Kirby cucumbers here, which do not require peeling.

QUICK-SAUTÉED GARLIC & SESAME CUCUMBERS

½ pound Persian or Kirby cucumbers, unpeeled (2 to 3 small cucumbers)

¼ teaspoon salt, or more to taste

1 tablespoon sesame oil

2 teaspoons minced garlic (about 2 cloves)

1 scallion, thinly sliced (about 2 tablespoons)

(ingredients continue)

1 Slice the cucumbers in half lengthwise, then into 1-inch pieces. Place the pieces cut-side down on a cutting board. Working with a few pieces at a time, lay the broad side of a wide chef's knife or cleaver on top of the cucumbers, and carefully use the palm of your free hand to smash down lightly on the blade. The pieces should crack and split open, leaving more surface area for the seasonings to flavor them. Place the smashed cucumbers in a shallow bowl and sprinkle them evenly with the salt. Set aside until cucumbers release water, 20 to 30 minutes. (Persian cucumbers may not release much.)

2 When the cucumbers are done brining, drain off any water that has collected. In a small saucepan, heat the sesame oil over medium-low until it rolls easily around the pan. Add the garlic and scallion; they should sizzle gently when they hit the pan. Sauté for about 30 seconds, until the garlic and scallion are fragrant. Add the cucumbers and stir for 10 to 20 seconds, until just combined and the cucumbers are warm. Adjust seasonings to taste and serve immediately.

(recipe continues)

SMASHED CUCUMBERS WITH VINEGAR, SESAME & SOY

½ pound Persian or Kirby cucumbers, unpeeled (2 to 3 small cucumbers)

¼ teaspoon salt, or more to taste

1 to 2 teaspoons rice vinegar

1 teaspoon sesame oil

½ to 1 teaspoon soy sauce

¼ to ½ teaspoon crushed red pepper flakes (optional)

1 Slice the cucumbers in half lengthwise, then into 1-inch pieces. Place the pieces cut-side down on a cutting board. Working with a few pieces at a time, lay the broad side of a wide chef's knife or cleaver on top of the cucumbers, and carefully use the palm of your free hand to smash down lightly on the blade. The pieces should crack and split open, leaving more surface area for the seasonings to flavor them. Place the smashed cucumbers in a shallow bowl and sprinkle them evenly with the salt. Set aside until cucumbers release water, 20 to 30 minutes. (Persian cucumbers may not release much.)

2 When the cucumbers are done brining, drain off any water that has collected. Stir in 1 teaspoon rice vinegar, 1 teaspoon sesame oil, ½ teaspoon soy sauce, and red pepper flakes (if using). Taste and adjust seasonings, if desired. Let sit at room temperature or in the refrigerator for 30 minutes to 1 hour to let the flavors combine.

NOTES

If using larger, thicker-skinned cucumbers, feel free to peel them.

EASIEST SESAME-SOY SALAD

Serves 2 as a larger salad, or 4 as a side

The Chinese cuisine I grew up eating almost never included the big bowls of leafy greens I now associate with "salad," but more often featured small plates of lightly dressed cucumbers (page 180), wood ear mushrooms, thin slices of lotus root, or cold jellyfish. Still, this is a salad that I learned from my very Chinese grandmother when she moved to the States to live with us. It was the only way I ever saw her eat lettuce, and I suspect that it was her method of bringing leafy raw greens, which must have seemed foreign to her, into familiar territory. It's hardly a recipe, really nothing more than a way to throw together a vibrant, flavorful bowl of greens when you realize you're all out of salad dressing, but I still love it for its minimalist simplicity and big flavor. I think of it as a Chinese twist on drizzling olive oil and vinegar on salad, and I like it best with a runny soft-boiled egg on top.

___

Divide the leafy greens into 2 to 4 bowls, followed by the tomatoes, scallions, cucumbers, carrots, and egg halves. Drizzle soy sauce, sesame oil, and black vinegar (if using) over each bowl, and serve.

4 cups leafy greens of your choice

½ cup cherry tomatoes, halved (about 8 cherry tomatoes)

¼ cup sliced scallions (2 to 3 scallions)

¼ cup julienned Persian or Kirby cucumbers, unpeeled (about ½ small cucumber)

¼ to ½ cup julienned carrots (about ¼ to ½ carrot)

2 soft-boiled eggs (any size), peeled and halved

3 to 4 teaspoons soy sauce

2 to 3 teaspoons sesame oil

1 to 2 teaspoons Chinkiang black vinegar (optional)

TEA EGGS

Makes 6 eggs; easily doubled (or tripled!)

6 eggs (any size)

¼ cup soy sauce

1 tablespoon loose-leaf black tea or 1 tea bag

2 to 3 whole star anise

1 stick cinnamon or ½ teaspoon ground cinnamon

½ teaspoon salt

½ teaspoon orange zest (optional)

1 teaspoon Sichuan or regular peppercorns (optional)

When I began to cook for myself in law school, I discovered how very easy these savory, lip-smacking Chinese street snacks were to make at home, and I went through a brief stint where I made them every week in droves. I shared them with hallmates; I peeled them at my desk while studying and tucked them into the fridge to snack on all week. The only problem was that our communal kitchen was through two sets of locked double doors from my dorm room, too far to hear much of anything that happens there, and as it turns out, fatigue from late-night studying and absentminded cooking do not always mix. My tea egg obsession came to an explosive halt one night when I left the pot on to boil, went back to my room, and—yes—fell asleep until the next morning.

So, please don't do that. And if you do, pray that, as in my case, the student who lives across the hall from the kitchen will hear your eggs exploding in the pot and remove them from the stove before any real damage is done.

---

1 Place the eggs in small pot filled with enough cold water that the eggs are covered by about 1 inch. Bring the water to a boil, then remove from the heat and cover. Let sit for 8 to 10 minutes to cook the eggs, then drain and rinse the eggs with cold water until cool enough to handle. Take each egg and tap it gently with the blunt end of a knife or the back of a spoon until the entire surface is lightly cracked. If small pieces flake off, don't worry, but do try to keep the shell intact over the egg.

2 Return the eggs to the pot. Add the soy sauce, tea, star anise, cinnamon, salt, and orange zest and peppercorns (if using), then add enough water to cover the eggs—usually about 4 cups or so—and give it a good stir.

3 Bring the mixture to a boil, then reduce the heat to medium-low and simmer for about 1 hour. For saltier, firmer eggs, continue to simmer for 2 or even 3 hours. (See Notes if you prefer eggs that are less well cooked.) Keep an eye on the liquid as it simmers; you may need to add water as the mixture boils down, aiming to keep the eggs submerged in broth. Serve warm or cold. The eggs will keep in the refrigerator for up to 1 week.

NOTES

Cooking the eggs this way will result in firm whites with well-cooked yolks that often have a green tinge around the edges. I don't mind them cooked this way, but if you prefer your eggs less well done, remove from the heat about 5 minutes after the mixture comes to a boil, and steep the eggs in the tea overnight instead. You could even take this one step further—in a brilliant idea I first learned from Mandy Lee of the food blog *Lady and Pups,* you can make soft-boiled tea eggs: (1) Boil your eggs to desired doneness; (2) rinse them and crack the shells; (3) boil the marinade ingredients—without the eggs—for about 5 minutes, just to let the flavors blend together, and let cool; (4) soak the eggs in the marinade overnight in the refrigerator.

GREEN BEANS & MINCED PORK

Serves 4 as a side

4 to 6 ounces ground pork

1 tablespoon soy sauce

1 tablespoon Shaoxing rice wine, dry sherry, or sake

1 teaspoon minced garlic (1 to 2 cloves)

½ teaspoon finely grated ginger root

1 teaspoon sugar (optional)

2 to 3 tablespoons vegetable oil or other neutral oil, divided

¼ teaspoon salt

⅛ teaspoon black pepper

1 pound fresh green beans, ends removed and snapped into 2- to 3-inch pieces

¼ cup chicken stock

1 cup sliced onions

2 to 3 tablespoons oyster sauce (teriyaki sauce works in a pinch)

Cooked rice, for serving

There are incarnations of wok-sautéed green beans and pork throughout different regions of Chinese cooking, with Sichuan-style "dry-fried" green beans perhaps one of the most popular. This one is my mother's homestyle version, which is a little lighter on oil and less finicky to prepare, but every bit as comfortingly hearty. It yields green beans that are tender and bright, with onions for sweetness, a dollop of oyster sauce for a lingering umami, and bits of savory pork laced throughout. I can never go more than a few weeks without making a big batch to enjoy—this, along with Chinese Scrambled Eggs & Tomatoes (page 195) and a big bowl of rice, is forever one of my favorite meals.

---

1 *Up to 1 hour ahead:* In a medium bowl, combine the pork, soy sauce, wine, garlic, ginger, and sugar (if using), and mix well. Cover and let marinate in the refrigerator while you prep the green beans.

2 *When you're ready to cook:* In a wok or large skillet, heat 1 tablespoon vegetable oil over high until shimmering. Add the ground pork and cook, breaking it up into small pieces, until browned, 3 to 4 minutes. Remove from the heat and set aside.

3 Wipe out the wok and return it to high heat. Add the remaining 1 to 2 tablespoons of oil (I like to use 2, but less is fine) and heat until shimmering. Add the salt and pepper, then the green beans, which should sizzle loudly as they hit the oil. Toss the beans vigorously with a spatula until the beans are evenly coated with oil and they begin to turn bright green, 2 to 3 minutes. Add the chicken stock, reduce the heat to medium-low, and cover. Let steam until the beans begin to soften but are not yet tender, about 3 minutes.

4 Uncover and increase the heat to medium-high. Add the sliced onions and ground pork and stir again until well combined. Reduce heat to medium-low and cover again for another 5 to 8 minutes, until the beans are tender. Add the oyster sauce (you may want to start with less, as it can be salty) and toss to coat the bean mixture. Adjust the seasonings, and serve with rice.

GINGER SHRIMP & GREEN PEAS

Serves 4

Before my mother taught me how to make this dish I'd always been intimidated, for some reason, by the idea of cooking shrimp. But in truth, there's nothing at all to fear. Once your shrimp are peeled and deveined (which you can do yourself, or simply buy them already prepped), just pop them in a quick marinade with lots of zingy ginger and white pepper, a bit of tenderizing cornstarch, and a splash of cooking wine to cut any fishy flavors. Flash-fry them in a searing-hot wok until pink and juicy, along with a heap of tender green peas, and you have dinner on the table. The sauce, which gets its flavor almost solely from the sweet shrimp, accentuated but not overshadowed by bright ginger, is the best part.

---

1 In a large bowl, combine the shrimp, rice wine, ginger, garlic, salt, and pepper, and stir until ingredients are thoroughly distributed. Sprinkle the cornstarch over the mixture and stir again until evenly coated. Cover and marinate in the refrigerator for 30 minutes to 1 hour.

2 In a large wok or skillet, heat the vegetable oil over high until shimmering and very hot. Add the scallions and cook briefly, just until fragrant, 20 to 30 seconds. Add the shrimp—the wok should sizzle loudly—and cook, tossing with a spatula every so often, until the shrimp are pink, about 5 minutes. Turn the heat off and add the peas, chili garlic paste, and vinegar (if using). Stir to incorporate, and serve immediately.

NOTES

My mother likes to slice her ginger and keep it in large pieces. Because I always find myself inadvertently chomping into an extra-spicy slice, I prefer to grate mine instead, so that it melts into everything else around it.

1 pound shrimp, peeled and deveined (tail on, if desired)

2 tablespoons Shaoxing rice wine, dry sherry, or sake

1 tablespoon finely grated ginger root

1 teaspoon minced garlic (1 to 2 cloves)

½ teaspoon salt

¼ teaspoon white pepper

1 teaspoon cornstarch

1 tablespoon vegetable oil or other neutral oil

¼ cup sliced scallions (2 to 3 scallions)

½ cup green peas (if frozen, thawed to room temperature)

½ to 1 teaspoon chili garlic paste (optional)

½ teaspoon Chinkiang black vinegar (optional)

GARLICKY BOK CHOY

Serves 4 as a side

2 tablespoons vegetable oil or other neutral oil

3 garlic cloves, thinly sliced or minced

1½ pounds Shanghainese or baby bok choy (6 to 8 bunches), ends trimmed

¼ cup chicken stock

Salt and black pepper, to taste

Cooked rice, for serving

As with most kids, I imagine, it wasn't until I started my own family that I appreciated exactly how much my mother did for us growing up. Where quick pastas or baked casseroles are sometimes all I manage to throw together, the kinds of dinners my mother put on the table never cease to amaze me even (or especially) now—there was always a meat main, two or more vegetables, even sometimes a soup afterward. I can still picture my mother chopping vegetables, starting her preparation hours before dinner. And I can imagine how a dish like this one might have been a relief for her in getting one more dish on the table that was not only quick, nearly hands-off, and wonderfully easy, but full of rich flavor and nutrition. Bok choy is delicious all on its own, tender dark leaves and soft roots, but when tossed in a wok with garlic-infused oil and steamed in chicken stock, it becomes even more flavorful, ready to accompany any main dish over a bowl of white rice.

---

1 In a large wok or skillet, heat the vegetable oil over high until shimmering and very hot. Add the garlic and cook briefly, just until fragrant, 30 seconds or less. Add the bok choy—it should sizzle very loudly as it hits the oil. Sauté briefly, tossing the bok choy vigorously, until evenly coated in oil.

2 Add the chicken stock, reduce the heat to low, and cover. Let steam until the bok choy stems are tender and the leaves are dark green and wilted, about 5 minutes. Season with salt and pepper, and serve hot, with rice.

CHINESE SCRAMBLED EGGS & TOMATOES

Serves 4 as a side

My husband tells me that he grew up eating his scrambled eggs with ketchup, but it wasn't until I got to college that I'd ever heard of that combination. My initial reaction was surprise, and a little bit of distaste. Ketchup and eggs? But then I realized I'd grown up eating that very same dish in a slightly different costume, in my mother's scrambled eggs and jammy, soft tomatoes. And after all, you need only look so far as *shakshuka*, or Spicy Gochujang Eggs in Purgatory (page 50), to realize that tomatoes and eggs are a classic combination. (Also, ketchup on eggs is actually delicious.)

Scrambled eggs and tomatoes is a classic Chinese dish that has appeared on my childhood dining table more times than I can count. Tomatoes are cooked until soft and sweet and mixed into creamy scrambled eggs, and the combination of savory, tangy, and slightly sweet, the interplay of textures between the egg curds and soft tomatoes, is the epitome of comfort food when mixed into a bowl of rice. I can think of nothing better when you're hungry and running low on supplies in the refrigerator.

1 Whisk the eggs and ¼ teaspoon salt together until very well combined, 1 to 2 minutes. Set aside.

2 In a medium skillet or large wok, heat a tablespoon of oil over medium-high. Add the tomatoes, sugar (if using), pepper, and another ⅛ to ¼ teaspoon salt, and cook until the skins wrinkle and the tomatoes soften and release liquid, 3 to 4 minutes. Remove from the pan and set aside. Wipe out the pan.

3 In the same pan, heat another tablespoon of oil over high until shimmering. Add the beaten eggs; they should immediately sizzle in the pan. Cook briefly until a layer of egg forms on the bottom of the pan, 30 seconds to 1 minute, then use a large spatula or wooden spoon to push the cooked layer to the side, letting the uncooked egg flow underneath so that a new layer of egg can cook. This creates crepe-y layers of scrambled eggs; it's not essential, but it's a nice texture. Repeat until most of the egg is cooked but it's still liquid in spots. Add the cooked tomatoes. Stir until combined, breaking the eggs into smaller pieces, and leave on the heat until the eggs are fully cooked. Adjust seasonings and serve immediately with rice.

6 large eggs, beaten

½ teaspoon salt, or to taste, divided

1 to 2 tablespoons vegetable oil or other neutral oil, divided

2 cups tomato wedges or halved grape or cherry tomatoes (I like a mix)

1 to 2 teaspoons sugar (optional)

⅛ teaspoon black pepper

Cooked rice, for serving

NOTES

This is best, as with most tomato dishes, when tomatoes are in season and at their sweetest. When I make it in the winter, I like to add a teaspoon or two of sugar; using grape or cherry tomatoes also goes a long way in adding a little bit of sweetness.

EASY BRAISED KABOCHA SQUASH

Serves 6 to 8 as a side

1 to 2 tablespoons
neutral oil

8 to 10 cups cubed
kabocha, washed well with
skin intact (about 1 small
2- to 3-pound squash)

½ cup sliced scallions
(3 to 4 scallions)

½ cup chicken broth

Salt, to taste

⅛ to ¼ teaspoon black
pepper

Kabocha squash was something new and novel, introduced to me when it became all the rage a few years ago as a sweeter, more flavorful cousin to pumpkin. Yet when I came home during the holidays and announced my newfound love for it to my mother, she looked at me with surprise and replied, "That's just Japanese pumpkin." I realized then that I'd been eating it for years. The way my mother makes it, sautéeing it briefly then simmering it in chicken stock, with plenty of salt and black pepper and a generous handful of scallions, results in a perfect balance of sweet, tender squash cloaked in a deeply savory broth, a meal all by itself or served with white rice.

1 In a large wok or skillet, heat the oil over high. Add the kabocha and scallions and toss with a spatula until the vegetables are evenly coated in oil.

2 Add the chicken broth and turn the heat to medium-low. Simmer, covered, until the kabocha is tender and cooked through, 10 to 15 minutes. Season with salt and pepper before serving.

FRIED KIMCHI

Serves 4 to 6 as a side

My mother-in-law, a tiny sprite of a Korean woman who barely cracks four foot eleven, might be the most cheerful person I've ever met. She is like most Asian mothers in that one of her greatest joys is making sure her children eat well, but her commitment to this higher calling is higher than most, I think, especially when her son and her daughter are visiting from their new faraway homes on the mainland. From the time they (and I) arrive until the time everyone leaves, there's food on the counter, food in the fridge, food on platters stealthily left outside their bedroom doors, often with the cutest cocktail forks. I'd like to grow up to be her.

For her son, my mother-in-law makes *jangjorim* (page 139), kimchi fried rice (page 113), and Spicy Shoyu Poke (page 93), and since I tag along with him on most trips, these are the dishes I most frequently enjoy. But on our first trip back at the same time as my sister-in-law, I came into the kitchen one day to find a pot bubbling away with nothing but, it appeared, kimchi. It was fried kimchi, I was told, just a glug of oil and a healthy pile of kimchi, cooked down to a fiery red, but from my first bite I was so in love that it was all I could do not to impolitely steal the whole batch from my sister-in-law. Cooked kimchi is probably something of a gateway to kimchi, if you find the fresh variety a bit too pungent. Fresh kimchi is sharp and brightly tart, but when cooked down, all the flavor from its brine, the salt and the fish sauce, are brought forward, resulting in a deeply savory, spicier side dish. My mother-in-law makes it and packs it into a Glasslock container in the fridge, where my sister-in-law (and now I) are free to sneak into it and have it over rice whenever we like. It usually doesn't last a day.

In a large skillet or saucepan, heat the oil over medium-high until shimmering. Add the kimchi and spread it into an even layer in the pan. Reduce the heat to medium and cook, stirring occasionally, until the kimchi liquid reduces and the whiter cabbage pieces turn slightly translucent and tinged red, 5 to 8 minutes. Serve warm or cold, with rice.

2 to 3 tablespoons vegetable or canola oil

2 cups roughly chopped kimchi, with liquid (about 2 to 3 tablespoons liquid)

Cooked rice, for serving

QUICK SWEET & SOUR CUCUMBER KIMCHI

Serves 2 or 3 as a side

1½ cups sliced Persian or Kirby cucumbers, unpeeled (2 to 3 small cucumbers or ½ pound)

¼ teaspoon salt, or more to taste

2 tablespoons thinly sliced scallions (about 1 scallion)

2 teaspoons rice vinegar

2 teaspoons gochugaru, or more to taste

1 teaspoon sugar

1 teaspoon sesame oil

Sesame seeds, for garnish (optional)

In cooking and eating Korean food with my husband's family, I was surprised to find that kimchi, which so usually connotes that briny, funky fermented cabbage packed into imposing jars, actually encompasses all varieties of pickled vegetables. There is water kimchi called *dongchimi*, mild, white, and sweet; mustard kimchi called *gat kimchi*; kimchi made from scallions; kimchi made from small stuffed Kirby cucumbers. This quick "kimchi," in turn, is often not called kimchi at all, and is more directly translated from its Korean name, *oi-muchim*, as "seasoned cucumbers." It is served as a small side dish, or *banchan*. I like it best when it is sweet, tangy from rice vinegar, and brightly spicy from *gochugaru*. It's one of the easiest side dishes I know, and one of the best.

Place the cucumber slices in a shallow bowl and sprinkle them evenly with salt. Let sit until water has collected in the bottom of the bowl, 20 to 30 minutes. (Persian cucumbers may not release much.) Drain the liquid, then add the scallions, rice vinegar, gochugaru, sugar, and sesame oil, and mix until very well combined and the sugar has dissolved. Adjust seasonings if needed, then let sit for 30 minutes to 1 hour to allow the flavors meld. Serve, garnished with sesame seeds, if desired.

KOREAN CHEESY CORN

Serves 3 or 4 as a side

The first time I had this dish was at a Boston outpost of the Korean fried chicken restaurant Bonchon. There, they call it "Corn Butter," but it's also known at other Korean barbecue joints as "cheese corn," and I once saw someone describe it as a Korean version of creamed corn, which I think is just right. In essence it is nothing more than sweet corn, cooked soft and creamy, tucked under a bubbling blanket of cheese that melts, decadent and rich, into the corn once you dig into it with a spoon. I dreamed about it for years after I had it before realizing that it's actually wonderfully easy to make right at home. You could even just stir in mozzarella to some roasted corn (which I'll admit we've done in the past and completely enjoyed), but this version is my favorite incarnation.

Preheat the oven to 500°F. In a large cast-iron or nonstick skillet, heat the oil until shimmering. Add the corn, salt, and pepper, and cook, stirring frequently, until fragrant and softened, 4 to 5 minutes. Transfer the corn to an ovenproof dish and stir in the mayonnaise. Sprinkle the mozzarella evenly across the top and bake for about 5 minutes, until the cheese is melted and bubbling. Top with scallions and cilantro and serve immediately.

1 tablespoon vegetable oil or other neutral oil, or unsalted butter

1½ cups sweet corn, fresh or frozen (if fresh, from about 2 ears)

¼ teaspoon salt

¼ teaspoon black pepper

2 tablespoons mayonnaise

½ cup (2 ounces) shredded mozzarella cheese

¼ cup sliced scallions (2 to 3 scallions), for garnish

¼ cup coarsely torn cilantro, for garnish

CREAMED CORN

Serves 4 as a side

3 cups sweet corn kernels, frozen or fresh (if fresh, from about 4 ears)

2 cups water

6 tablespoons sugar

1 teaspoon salt, plus more to taste

¼ cup heavy cream

1 tablespoon unsalted butter

Black pepper, to taste

This creamed corn is inspired by one of my favorite restaurants back home. It's the same restaurant that dishes up my dad's go-to baby-back ribs, and their creamed corn is just as good—unapologetically rich and sweet, full to the brim with pure summer corn sunshine. The secret is to purée *some* of the corn, but not all of it, which lets the corn flavor shine while still maintaining the texture from its kernels, and creates a creamy, almost pudding-like texture that doesn't use nearly as much cream or butter as you would think. It's the essence of corn, and the essence of summer decadence, in one bright little cup.

In a medium saucepan, combine the corn, water, sugar, and salt, and bring to a boil. Simmer until the corn is soft and cooked through, 6 to 8 minutes. Drain and add about half the corn to a blender with the cream and butter. Purée just briefly, until partly smooth, 10 to 20 seconds. Stir the purée and remaining corn kernels together in a bowl, and season with salt and pepper. Serve immediately.

PIMENTO CHEESE MACARONI SALAD

Serves 6 to 8 as a side

I had no idea that pimento cheese was uniquely Southern until I left the South and, hit by a sudden craving in the middle of Manhattan, discovered that my beloved tangy, creamy spread was scarcely anywhere to be found. Luckily, jarred pimento peppers usually *can* be found anywhere, and so homemade pimento cheese is only a few ingredients away, no matter where you are. Made from a generous dose of mayonnaise, pungent sharp cheddar, and sweet pimento peppers, with just a hint of cayenne to give it a pop, it's as good on plain, soft Wonder Bread as it is here, where I've mixed it into a childhood barbecue side from my husband's Hawaii childhood—macaroni salad, or the efficiently nicknamed "mac salad." It's a bouncy, creamy, cheesy, and utterly shameless carbs-on-carbs take on summer ersatz "salads." I'll admit it: I still like it sandwiched between soft white bread.

---

1 Bring a pot of well-salted water to a boil (I use about 2 teaspoons salt in a quart or so of water). Add the macaroni and cook until your desired doneness. Drain and let cool completely, about 30 minutes.

2 Meanwhile, in a large bowl, combine the cheese, diced pimentos, and mayonnaise. Season with salt, sugar, cayenne, and black pepper (you might want to add these to taste, though the amounts I've listed are what I prefer) and mix in the macaroni.

3 Cover and chill in the fridge for a few hours, ideally overnight, to let the flavors come together. Serve as a side, a dip, or a sandwich spread.

NOTES

For traditional Southern pimento cheese spread, use 8 ounces of cheese and omit the macaroni.

2½ teaspoons salt, or more to taste

2 cups (8 ounces) dried elbow macaroni

1½ cups (6 ounces) shredded extra-sharp cheddar cheese

½ cup jarred, drained diced pimento peppers (often labeled "pimiento peppers"; if you can't find them, jarred roasted red bell peppers work in a pinch)

½ cup mayonnaise

½ teaspoon sugar

⅛ to ¼ teaspoon cayenne pepper (or more if you like heat)

Pinch of black pepper

SESAME-MISO POTATO SALAD

Serves 3 or 4; easily doubled

FOR THE POTATOES

2 pounds baby red or fingerling potatoes, scrubbed and cut into ¾-inch cubes (Red Bliss or other waxy potatoes work well, too)

1 tablespoon salt

2 tablespoons rice vinegar

FOR THE DRESSING

⅓ cup mayonnaise

¼ cup full-fat Greek yogurt

2 to 3 tablespoons white miso paste, room temperature (see Notes)

1 teaspoon sesame oil

1 to 2 teaspoons honey, to taste (optional)

¼ teaspoon salt, or more to taste

¼ teaspoon black pepper, or more to taste

TO ASSEMBLE

1½ cups trimmed and thinly sliced sugar snap peas (see Notes)

¼ cup diced shallots or red onion (about 1 shallot or ¼ onion)

4 large hard-boiled eggs, peeled and sliced

⅓ cup finely sliced scallions (about 3 scallions), for garnish

⅓ cup coarsely chopped cilantro, for garnish (optional)

My ideal potato salad, the kind that keeps me coming back to the picnic spread for just one more spoonful, and then one more, is cool, creamy, and ever-so-slightly sweet and tangy. It should be generous with the mayonnaise, full of lively textures from a confetti of crunchy vegetables and bouncy hard-boiled eggs in contrast to the tender, silky potatoes. This recipe is a twist on the standard, but it still ticks off every one of those boxes. There's sweet sugar snap peas, sliced thin like cheerful little vegetal polka dots, for plenty of crunch; miso paste for a fermented, salty undertone; sesame oil for nuttiness; and scallions and cilantro for brightness. If you don't have miso paste on hand, this can easily be made into a typical potato salad, with mayonnaise, a bit of nose-tickling mustard, and herbs.

---

1 Place the potatoes and salt in a pot with enough cold water to cover them by 1 inch. Bring to a boil and reduce the heat to medium. Simmer until a fork slides through the potatoes without resistance, 7 to 8 minutes.

2 Drain the potatoes and transfer them to a large bowl. Add the vinegar and toss gently with a silicone spatula to combine. Let stand until the potatoes are cool, about 30 minutes.

3 Meanwhile, in a small bowl, whisk together the mayonnaise, yogurt, miso paste, sesame oil, honey (if using), salt, and pepper until smooth. Using a silicone spatula, gently fold the sugar snap peas, shallots, and eggs into the potatoes, then fold in about two-thirds of the dressing. If it is too dry for your taste, add the remaining dressing until it reaches your desired consistency. Cover and refrigerate until chilled, about 1 hour. Serve cold, with scallions and cilantro on top, if desired. The potato salad can be covered and kept refrigerated for up to 1 day.

(recipe continues)

NOTES

Miso paste is becoming more widely available in supermarkets these days; for this salad, look for white or yellow miso, which is sweet and has a mild flavor. If all you have is a darker miso, though, you'll be just fine with that, too—just use a little bit less. Note that miso paste at room temperature is easier to whisk and incorporate into the other ingredients.

If you can't find miso paste, this is just as good prepared as a standard potato salad: simply replace the miso with 2 to 3 teaspoons mustard, add 2 to 3 tablespoons sweet pickle relish, and swap out the cilantro for minced fresh parsley and/or dill leaves. A ½ cup or so of diced celery makes for a crunchy addition, too.

Use tender, sweet sugar snap peas here and avoid any that are too tough.

WEEKNIGHT ASPARAGUS

Serves 3 or 4 as a side

Of the myriad ways to prepare this stunning springtime vegetable—braised in butter, rolled in bread crumbs, roasted—I always find myself coming back to this one. It's the way my mother prepares asparagus, and it's a method that might already be familiar if you've made the Garlicky Bok Choy (page 192) or Easy Braised Kabocha Squash (page 196). This asparagus is impossibly tender and flavorful, its fragrant and savory flavor allowed to sing undiluted, and it couldn't be simpler, quicker, or more delicious.

1 pound asparagus, woody ends trimmed

2 tablespoons vegetable oil or other neutral oil

½ teaspoon salt, or to taste

¼ teaspoon black pepper, or to taste

3 to 4 tablespoons chicken broth

---

1 Slice the asparagus into 2-inch pieces and set aside. In a large wok or skillet, heat the oil over high until shimmering. Add the asparagus—it should sizzle nice and loud—and season generously with salt and pepper. Toss the asparagus with a spatula until it is well coated in oil and gets a bit of a sear on some sides. It doesn't need to be browned but should begin to become fragrant after 30 seconds or so.

2 Reduce the heat to medium-low and add the chicken broth. Cover and let steam until the asparagus is tender, about 10 minutes.

SWEET SESAME SKILLET CORNBREAD

Makes a 10-inch round cornbread, enough to feed 6 to 8 (or more)

Cornbread is a subject of vigorous debate in the South, and whether to add sugar is especially particularly divisive. Given that my family only recently immigrated to the South, the reason I love sugar in my cornbread isn't because it's the way my family has always done it, but simply because it's what I like. As a result of having little tradition to anchor me to how cornbread "should" be, but loving it all the same, I've slowly come to a version that is unabashedly untraditional, sidestepping all debates about sugar and landing on a quirky recipe that has just a bit of Eastern influence. It is plenty sweet, of course, but also subtly smoky and nutty from sesame seeds. You can brush more sesame oil on after baking to bring out the flavor even more strongly, or you can serve it with butter and a bit of honey—this is no traditional cornbread, after all, so it's all up to you.

---

1 Preheat the oven to 350°F. Generously brush a 10-inch cast-iron skillet with butter and place it in the oven while the oven preheats.

2 Meanwhile, in a large bowl, whisk together the cornmeal, flour, sesame seeds, sugar, baking powder, baking soda, and salt. In a separate small bowl or liquid measuring cup, whisk together the milk, Greek yogurt, eggs, melted butter, and 4 tablespoons of the honey. Add the wet ingredients to the dry and mix just until combined. The batter will be lumpy.

3 When the oven is hot, remove the skillet and pour in the batter. It should sizzle. Bake for 25 to 30 minutes, or until the edges just begin to pull away from the sides of the skillet, the center of the cornbread bounces back when touched, and a cake tester or toothpick inserted in the center of the cornbread comes out clean.

4 While the cornbread is baking, whisk together the remaining tablespoon honey and the sesame oil. When the cornbread is done, remove from oven and brush the honey-sesame oil mixture evenly over the top. Sprinkle with additional sesame seeds and serve warm, with more butter or sesame oil, if desired.

6 tablespoons (¾ stick) unsalted butter, melted, plus more to grease the skillet and for serving (optional)

1 cup yellow cornmeal

1 cup (125 grams) all-purpose flour

¼ cup toasted sesame seeds, plus more for garnish

¼ cup sugar

1 teaspoon baking powder

½ teaspoon baking soda

1 teaspoon salt

¾ cup whole milk

¾ cup full-fat Greek yogurt (or use 1½ cups buttermilk in place of the milk and yogurt)

2 large eggs

5 tablespoons honey, divided

1 tablespoon sesame oil

SWEET

ASIAN PEAR & JASMINE CRUMBLE

Makes 2 to 4 individual crumbles, depending on the size of your ramekins

My earliest memories of Asian pears are from my grandparents' kitchen in a concrete high-rise in bustling Shanghai, sitting around an old, worn table under fluorescent lights after a long flight from the United States. Asian pears are meant to be eaten peeled, and I can still see the ribbons of peels as they curled off my grandmother's paring knife, seamless, swift, and unbroken, piling around the slices as she set them before us. (To my mother's dismay, this is not a skill I have ever mastered.)

These little individual desserts are a combination of nostalgia for my childhood trips to Shanghai and my summers back in South Carolina—here, those late-night Asian pears are combined with the tea that followed every family dinner, then baked into a warm, buttery, gently spiced crumble that I associate with cookouts in the South. The result is familiar yet excitingly new, heady with the floral mixture of jasmine and pear, but sweetly comforting from the crunchy crumble topping. It is my favorite kind of foray into blending the various influences from my childhood.

---

1 *Make the jasmine-soaked pears:* Place the tea in a medium bowl. Bring the water to a boil and pour it over the tea. Let steep for about 10 minutes, until very strong.

2 In the meantime, core and dice the pear. Add the diced pear and sugar to the tea. Stir to dissolve the sugar, then cover and let soak in the refrigerator for 1 to 2 hours, or up to overnight for best results. Alternatively, if you're pressed for time, simmer the pear with the tea and sugar in a small pot over low heat for about 20 minutes, until the pear tastes strongly of jasmine tea, then let cool. This will result in a softer crumble, but it will do just fine.

3 *Make the crumble topping:* While the pear is soaking, preheat the oven to 350°F. In a medium bowl, combine the oats, flour, sugars, ground ginger, and salt. Using your fingers, mix in the butter until the mixture forms clumps the size of peas and the consistency resembles wet sand.

(recipe continues)

FOR THE JASMINE-SOAKED PEARS

3 to 4 tablespoons loose-leaf jasmine tea, or 3 or 4 jasmine tea bags (Ten Ren is a family favorite)

1½ cups water

1 large Asian pear, peeled (see Notes)

¼ cup sugar

FOR THE CRUMBLE TOPPING

3 tablespoons old-fashioned oats

3 tablespoons (about 25 grams) flour

3 tablespoons light brown sugar

2 tablespoons granulated sugar

¼ teaspoon ground ginger

⅛ teaspoon salt

3 tablespoons cold unsalted butter, diced

Vanilla ice cream, whipped cream, or yogurt, for serving

4 Remove the pear from the tea and divide between 2 and 4 oven-proof ramekins or mini cocottes, depending on the size of the containers. Divide the crumble topping evenly among the ramekins. Bake for 10 to 15 minutes, until the topping is browned and crisp and the filling is bubbling at the edges. Serve warm, with vanilla ice cream, whipped cream, or yogurt.

NOTES

Asian pears are fragrant and juicy, with a fresh crunch that sets them apart from Western pears. They're also a bit grainier, and the high water content usually makes them less attractive for baking from fresh. But the sweet floral quality is a perfect complement to jasmine tea, and when the pears are softened in tea overnight, they will release less water during baking and cook beautifully into the crumble.

You can find Asian pears in almost all Asian supermarkets, especially Korean and Chinese ones, and you'll even find a similar variety (sometimes called "apple pears") in some mainstream grocery stores now and again. If you can't track them down, though, Bosc or Bartlett pears will work just as well.

BLACK SESAME CHOCOLATE LOAF

Makes one 9 × 5-inch loaf

I first discovered a version of this squidgy, moist, intensely chocolatey loaf, which has its origins in a recipe by Nigella Lawson, through Sarah Kieffer's *The Vanilla Bean Baking Book*. I've really never had anything quite like it—inky black from all its chocolate, tender and beautifully moist, almost gooey yet still cake-like. Here, the addition of toasted and finely ground black sesame seeds takes a perfect thing and, dare I say, makes it even better. The black sesame brings an alluringly nutty, smoky, charcoal undertone to the cake that goes perfectly with the bittersweet chocolate, and the roughly ground seeds add a little bit of texture and crunch to the dense luxuriance of the cake. Serve it with whipped cream or mascarpone whisked with a little extra black sesame sugar for a deeply satisfying, grown-up take on cookies and cream. It's one of the best things I've ever made.

½ cup black sesame seeds

4 ounces bittersweet chocolate, chopped

1½ cups packed light brown sugar

1 cup (2 sticks) unsalted butter, softened

2 large eggs, beaten

½ teaspoon vanilla extract

1¼ cups (156 grams) all-purpose flour

1 teaspoon baking soda

1 cup boiling water or hot coffee

Whipped cream, mascarpone, or ice cream, for serving (optional)

1 Preheat the oven to 375°F. Grease and line a tall, 9 × 5-inch Pullman-style loaf pan with parchment paper. A regular height loaf pan may overflow—if this is all you have, take care to fill the pan less than 1 inch from the rim, and save the excess for muffins or mini cakes.

2 In a small, dry skillet, toast the black sesame seeds over medium heat until a few seeds jump in the pan and they start to smell toasty (but not burnt!), 2 to 3 minutes. Place in a food processor and blend until a finely ground powder forms, 1 to 2 minutes. Set aside.

3 Melt the chocolate, either in the microwave in 15 to 30 second increments, stirring between each interval, until fully melted and smooth, or over a double boiler for about 5 minutes, stirring frequently. Once the chocolate is melted, set aside and let cool slightly.

4 In a large bowl, cream together the brown sugar, butter, and sesame-seed powder until fluffy, 2 to 3 minutes with an electric mixer on medium speed or 3 to 4 minutes by hand. Add the eggs and vanilla, beating well. Fold in the melted chocolate until just incorporated.

(recipe continues)

5 In a medium bowl, whisk together the flour and baking soda. Alternate folding in the flour mixture and the hot water (or coffee), ¼ cup of each at a time, until the batter becomes smooth and liquidy.

6 Pour the batter into the lined loaf pan, taking care not to fill the pan higher than 1 inch from the rim.

7 Bake for 30 minutes, then reduce the heat to 325°F and continue baking for about 15 more minutes. The cake should still be relatively moist in the center, and a skewer or cake tester should not come out completely clean.

8 Remove from the oven and let cool completely before turning the cake out onto a plate. The cake may fall; this is normal, as it is so moist. Serve with whipped cream, mascarpone, or ice cream, if desired. The cake tastes even better on the second day.

NOTES

For a stronger black sesame flavor, use ¾ cup black sesame seeds.

the only way out is through (cooking)

ANDREW AND I SPENT MOST OF THE SUMMER after our graduation from law school studying for the bar exam, holed up in our apartment amid thick books and piles of notes. We faced down the dreaded test at the end of July, and between the end of the exam and my first day of full-time employment were a little more than ten glorious weeks of freedom. So, naturally, I spent the entire time cooking.

This was an oasis wholly untethered from responsibilities, the respite before we went out to become "real" lawyers, and we had all been regaled with horror stories of what life would be like in the assortment of skyscrapers destined to be our second homes. Quaking at the specter of all-nighters in the office or rushing in on weekends after urgent emails demanding work now-now-now, I thought, *Isn't this my last chance to make all the things I can, while I still can?*

The first third of our last "summer break" we spent in Hawaii with Andrew's family. In my mother-in-law's sun-drenched kitchen in Honolulu, the door to her *lanai* open and curtains fluttering lazily in the sunshine, I helped her blanch spinach and bean sprouts for bibimbap and dredge zucchini in flour and egg for *jeon*, which were by then familiar to me. We stirred chopped kimchi into mung bean batter until orange and spicy for *bindaetteok* (page 135), and I mystified her by sandwiching some of that kimchi into a grilled cheese (page 57).

Then across the country I went to my parents' kitchen in South Carolina, where my mother taught me to make the dishes I'd been waiting to learn—savory but surprisingly simple Braised Kabocha Squash (page 196); her Chinese "Russian" Soup (page 141), slow-simmered and layered with flavor; her secret filling for her delicate

wontons (see page 166). My dad, too, taught me recipes from his side of the family, like his beloved grandmother's Lion's Head Meatballs (page 152). In between, I made my first yeast bread, setting it on the porch on a warm South Carolina evening to watch it rise with awe.

Finally, when I got back to our apartment in Brooklyn, I christened it with cookies and cakes and pies, then ventured out to deliver them to anyone who wanted them or who, at least, wouldn't say no. I snapped photographs and posted it all to my burgeoning (and, I thought, soon to be extinct) blog, *Two Red Bowls*, and dropped onto the couch at the end of the day covered in flour and utterly pooped, convinced that I was one day closer to not having the time to do any of this again.

A few weeks later, I put on a suit and ventured into the steel-gray monolith that towered above Grand Central. I sat down in my office for the first time as a junior attorney, said hello to my new officemate, and began work.

But, as so often happens, what I had so thoroughly dreaded was nowhere near as bad as I'd feared. It was true, for most weeknights cooking was more difficult than before—I came home long after dinnertime on many days, and my husband, at another firm in the city, did, too. We grew accustomed to the ominous buzz of work phones and the tap-tap-tapping of one, or both, of us responding rapidly to a late-night email.

But I managed to steal lunch breaks here and there, which meant the whole of New York City's diverse food options was my oyster (well, the whole of New York's food that was under a certain dollar limit and a certain mile radius). And our weekends weren't disrupted as often as I imagined they'd be, leaving sleepy Saturday mornings and long afternoons for any ambitious baking project I could dream up.

In this "new normal," I spent my weekdays trying new things from different restaurants, skipping out for lunch on occasion to try the new Dough doughnut or a Roberta's pizza from the new food hall across the street, eating delivered soup dumplings or New York bagels in front of my computer in the evening and, in fits of procrastination, scribbling ideas for recipes for *Two Red Bowls* and Googling the foods I liked.

Either I discovered ways to make dinner more quickly, using roux cubes to make Japanese curry or portioning out Ziplocs of *jangjorim* (page 139) to freeze for later, or, on the weekends, I dove into long recipes that provided an unexpected respite from legal work. I shut my laptop and traded in brief-writing and legal research for notes on dough rise times and flour-to-water ratios. I kneaded dough as my own form of therapy on Friday nights, leaving it to rise overnight and baking it into lofty loaves (page 30) on Saturday mornings. I folded Potstickers (page 157) on quiet weekend afternoons, to be frozen and pan-fried the next day, and tried my hand at pasta from scratch, covering the kitchen in flour and sweating over wide sheets of yellow pappardelle. And I laid it all on a wide-planked wooden table by the tall windows in our coolly lit Brooklyn living room, hopped up on a chair, and snapped photos of it for the blog.

I assumed that once work started, *Two Red Bowls* would become a thing of the past. But even as this lawyering business grew busier, I found that *Two Red Bowls* only grew with it. The more that I worked, sometimes more than a little stressed and anxious, the more that I looked forward to the blog that had become my creative

outlet: the next meal I could eat that would inspire the next weekend project, the next way I could make something that I'd always loved but with less time or effort, and the next blog post filled with what I'd recently discovered.

I imagine this is what food is all about, in some ways—it reflects how life changes, even as one phase that you know "ends" and a new, often thrilling one begins. Just as the food we made changed when we stopped being students and started working, it changed when we moved from Brooklyn to Los Angeles three years later, where I found avocados year-round and Japanese sweet potatoes by the crateful. It changed again when our son was born, with nourishing Chinese and Korean postpartum soups for me in the days after he was born, and simple snacks for him to try as his first foods. The dishes we eat and make are always ready to be inspired by new experiences and new things, if we want them to be—just as much as they are inspired by the old experiences and the traditions that came before.

EGG CUSTARD STEAMED BUNS

Makes 18 to 20 buns

I grew up eating little frozen store-bought versions of these for breakfast. Popped in the microwave for 30 seconds or so, they came out steaming, soft, and puffy, but not for long—I'd scarf them down, mouth unattractively agape from their lava-hot innards, in my hurry to eat them before they turned cool and tough. You'll have no such problem when they're fresh out of your own steamer.

In developing the filling, I found that the majority of recipes I came across called for custard powder, which to me tasted slightly cloying and artificial. Why resort to the premade stuff? As it turns out, to get the creamy, gently sweet and comfortingly eggy filling I remembered from my childhood, it is traditional custard, made from sunny yellow egg yolks, sugar, cornstarch, and milk, that tastes truest and best.

1 batch Steamed Buns (page 64), prepared to the start of the first rise

1 cup whole milk (or heavy cream; if using cream, omit the butter)

2 tablespoons unsalted butter

4 large egg yolks

½ cup sugar

3 tablespoons cornstarch

2 teaspoons vanilla extract

---

1 *The night before, or at least 2 hours in advance:* Prepare 1 batch of the Steamed Buns (page 64) up to the start of the first rise.

2 *Meanwhile, make the custard:* Place the milk and butter in a 2-quart saucepan over medium heat. While it's warming, in a medium bowl or liquid measuring cup, whisk together the egg yolks, sugar, cornstarch, and vanilla.

3 When the butter has melted and the milk is bubbling around the edges, remove from the heat and pour a thin stream into the egg mixture, whisking vigorously as you do. When all of the hot cream has been whisked into the egg, return the mixture to the pot over medium heat. Cook, whisking continuously, until lines from the whisk begin to appear in the custard, 3 to 5 minutes. Reduce the heat to low and continue whisking until the custard reaches a pudding-like consistency, another 20 to 30 seconds. The resulting custard should be thick but pourable, and will thicken further upon chilling. Place the custard in the refrigerator until fully chilled, 30 minutes to 1 hour, or overnight.

(recipe continues)

4 *An hour or so before you'd like to make the buns:* Line a baking sheet with plastic wrap or parchment paper. Using a small ice cream scoop or a round spoon, drop 18 to 20 tablespoon-size dollops of custard onto the baking sheet. Cover with more plastic wrap and place the baking sheet in the freezer until the custard dollops are firm, 30 to 45 minutes.

5 Meanwhile, when the dough has risen, punch it down and knead a few times. Divide the dough into 18 to 20 equal pieces and cut out the same number of 4-inch parchment-paper squares. For each piece, roll the dough out to a 4- or 5-inch circle, aiming to roll the edges thinner than the center. Place a frozen custard dollop in the center and pinch the edges of the dough up around the filling to seal. Place the shaped bun seam-side down on a parchment square. Repeat until all the filling and all the dough is gone.

6 *Set up the steamer:* If using a pot with a steamer basket, fill the pot with plenty of water, about 2 quarts or so, and bring it to a boil over high heat. If using a bamboo steamer, fill a large wok or skillet with about 2 inches of water and bring to a boil over high heat. The water should be high enough that the bamboo steamer rim rests in the water, but not so high that the bottom of the basket touches the water.

7 Starting with the buns you shaped first, place 3 or 4 buns in each steamer tier, leaving a generous 2 to 3 inches between each bun. Reduce the heat to medium-low, or low enough to keep the water just at a gentle simmer, and set the steamer over the water, covered. Steam the buns until cooked through and resilient when touched, about 15 minutes. (You may want to place the remaining buns in the refrigerator to slow the rising while you steam the first batches.)

8 Repeat with the remaining buns. Serve warm. Leftovers can be frozen for up to 6 months and reheated in a steamer or microwave.

STICKY SESAME PEANUT PIE

Makes one 9-inch pie

I have a confession: I am that person who ate all the filling from underneath the pecans in that classically Southern and perfectly delicious pecan pie. I am the one who left the nuts behind, lonely and forlorn in the pie pan. For most of my childhood in the South, I had a love-hate relationship with pecan pie, smitten with its deeply warm, gooey filling but indifferent toward the nuts on top, which I usually found too bitter. Perhaps I just never found the right pie, but rather than embark on that journey, I found an unlikely but perfect solution in this quirky yet familiar confection.

This pie combines a nostalgic childhood Chinese candy, peanut sesame brittle, with all the things I love about classic pecan pie. It keeps the sweet, decadent traditional pie filling but swaps out the pecans for roasted peanuts and sesame seeds on top. It reminds me of both the candy and the pie, but with the volume turned all the way up: There's a layer of crunch from the sesame seeds and the peanuts, and underneath that there's a lot of the warm gooeyness that I love in pecan pie, all tucked into a buttery, flaky, irresistible pie crust.

---

1 *Parbake the pie crust:* Preheat the oven to 425°F. Lightly prick the bottom of the crust with a fork (taking care not to poke all the way through). Line the pie crust with parchment paper or buttered foil and fill with pie weights, dried beans, or pennies. Bake for 10 to 13 minutes, until the edges are lightly golden-brown. Remove the parchment paper and pie weights, then bake for 1 to 2 more minutes, until the bottom of the pie crust appears dry. Set the crust aside while you make the filling; reduce the heat to 350°F.

2 *Make the filling:* In a small saucepan, combine the brown sugar, corn syrup, and butter over medium heat. Cook, stirring continuously, until the butter melts and the mixture becomes a smooth syrup, free of any graininess. Remove from the heat and let cool for 5 to 10 minutes. Whisk in the eggs, vanilla, vinegar (if using), peanuts, and sesame seeds until evenly incorporated. Pour into the pie crust and bake at 350°F for 45 to 50 minutes, until the filling is puffy and barely jiggles when shaken. Cool completely before serving. The pie will keep, covered, in the refrigerator for several days. Enjoy with whipped cream, yogurt, or ice cream.

(recipe continues)

1 batch Pie Crust
(page 231), shaped in
the pan and frozen

1 cup packed dark brown
sugar

½ cup light corn syrup
(or, if you can find it,
golden syrup; see Notes)

6 tablespoons unsalted
butter

3 large eggs

2 teaspoons vanilla extract

1 teaspoon apple cider
vinegar (optional)

1 cup roasted peanuts

½ cup sesame seeds

Whipped cream,
Greek yogurt, or ice
cream, for serving

NOTES

I learned two fascinating things about pecan pie from Deb Perelman of *Smitten Kitchen*. The first is that apple cider vinegar is magical at cutting through the sometimes-cloying sweetness in the pie filling and adding a bit of depth. To me, the filling with a touch of vinegar added tasted beautifully of caramel, whereas the one without it tasted only of sweet. At the same time, my husband prefers the pie without the vinegar, so I've listed it as optional.

The second is that golden syrup can be substituted for corn syrup for a deeper, rounder flavor. I loved this discovery, as golden syrup, a common UK ingredient, is actually a sweetener often used in mooncakes and other sweets in Hong Kong. If you can find a bottle of Lyle's (Amazon is a good source), you should absolutely use it in place of corn syrup.

PIE CRUST

Makes one 10-inch deep-dish crust, one generous 9-inch standard pie crust,
or four 4-inch miniature crusts

Let me be the first to say that there is no shame at all in store-bought crusts, and if this will save you time and bring you joy in the kitchen, then by all means, opt for it. I will also say, though, that I never loved pie crust until I made my own from scratch. It is finicky, and often has a mind of its own in the oven, but the flaky, shattering, buttery result is always worth it.

For a long time, I used a pie crust recipe that called for 1¼ cups of flour and 1 stick of butter. But I found that upping the quantities just slightly made rolling the dough out far easier, giving a bit more wiggle room for any fissures that might rear their inconvenient heads, or any edges that end up a tad lopsided. The extra scraps are excellent baked all on their own, sprinkled with a little cinnamon and turbinado sugar.

1½ cups (187 grams) all-purpose flour, plus more for rolling

1 tablespoon sugar

½ teaspoon salt

½ cup plus 2 tablespoons (1¼ sticks) unsalted butter, frozen

¼ cup ice water, plus 1 to 2 tablespoons more if needed

1 Whisk together the flour, sugar, and salt in a bowl. Using the largest holes on a box grater, grate the frozen butter into the bowl, then mix with a wooden spoon or your fingers until pea-size crumbles form. Add ¼ cup ice water and stir until a crumbly dough forms. If needed, drizzle in more ice water, 1 tablespoon at a time, until a fistful of the dough holds together when squeezed. Gather and knead the dough together into a single disk. If it's unwieldy, pile the dough on a piece of plastic wrap and use the edges of the plastic wrap to gather the dough together. Wrap and chill in the refrigerator for at least 1 hour or up to 3 days.

2 On a well-floured surface or between two pieces of parchment paper (I prefer the floured surface, for ease), roll the dough ¼- to ⅛-inch thick. For me, the larger the piece of dough, the better. Overturn a pie pan onto the dough and use a knife to trace out a circle of dough about 3 inches larger than the pan's edges—for a 9-inch pie pan, about 12 inches in diameter. If using miniature pans, reroll the dough as needed and repeat.

3 Place the dough gently into the pie pan and nudge it into place. Try not to stretch it, which can lead to shrinking in the oven. There should be about a 1-inch overhang; tuck this underneath the rim of the pan to form a nice smooth edge, then use your fingers or a fork to crimp the edges. Place the formed crusts in the freezer until firm, 15 to 20 minutes, then use with the filling of your choice.

MATCHA-GLAZED SWIRL BREAD

Makes one 9 × 5-inch loaf

FOR THE SWEET DOUGH

¼ cup whole milk

¼ cup (½ stick) unsalted butter, plus more for pan

1 teaspoon active dry yeast or instant yeast (see Notes)

2¼ cups (282 grams) all-purpose flour, plus more for rolling

3 tablespoons granulated sugar

¼ teaspoon salt

1 large egg plus 1 large egg yolk, lightly beaten

¼ cup full-fat Greek yogurt (see Notes)

½ teaspoon vanilla extract

FOR THE MATCHA GLAZE

1 tablespoon plus 1 teaspoon matcha powder

5 tablespoons heavy cream, plus 1 teaspoon more for thinning

1¼ cups confectioners' sugar

TO FINISH

All-purpose flour, for rolling

The department stores in Japan usually have majestic food halls on their basement level, and the Daimaru department store in Kyoto is no different. My favorite spot there is the Paul Bocuse Bakery, filled to bursting with arrays of every baked good you could imagine, from sticky slices of bruléed custard bread to savory ham-and-egg buns. This was where I found a gem that has stayed with me from my first bite all the way to writing this cookbook—a loaf of intricately swirled bread filled with matcha glaze and draped with the same alluring glaze on top. The bread was shaped like four giant cinnamon rolls cozied together in a loaf pan, but with many, many more layers, all beautifully laced with matcha glaze. I bought a half-loaf, and loved it so much that I convinced my husband to go back with me to buy a full one the very next day.

Being thousands of miles away from that fantastic bakery, it was only a matter of time before I felt the need to try to make this at home. For once my compulsive need to take pictures of food paid off grandly. Armed with photos (of the full loaf, of one section, of a cross-section, of the loaf the day after) I inspected them, baked my own loaf, inspected the photos again, baked another loaf, et cetera, until I finally came up with something that I love nearly as much. The dough is based on my favorite dough for cinnamon rolls (page 241), a sweet one enriched with plenty of butter and egg, and pillowy from an extra-long overnight rise, rolled out as thin as I can possibly get it and slathered with matcha glaze. The very thin layers make for a slightly unpredictable loaf that tends to turn out (much like the bakery version) a bit lopsided—but I think that just adds to the charm.

---

1 *The night before, or at least 2 hours before baking:* In a small saucepan over medium heat, bring the milk just to a boil, 2 to 3 minutes, or heat the milk in a small microwave-safe bowl in the microwave, about 1 minute. (This scalds the milk to kill any enzymes that might prevent the yeast from doing their thing.) If you find a film on the surface of the milk after heating it, just pour the milk through a sieve. Add the butter and stir until melted. Let the mixture cool slightly until warm to the touch but not hot, about 100°F to 110°F. Sprinkle the yeast on top and let sit until foamy, 5 to 10 minutes. If the milk-yeast mixture does not foam, you may want to start over to make sure your yeast is active. (See Notes if using instant yeast.)

(recipe continues)

2 Meanwhile, in a large bowl, whisk together the flour, granulated sugar, and salt. If not using a scale, take care to use the spoon-and-sweep method for measuring your flour (page 19), since too much flour can make the dough dense.

3 When the yeast is foamy, add the egg and egg yolk, yogurt, and vanilla to the yeast-milk mixture and whisk to combine. Mix the wet ingredients into the dry, until all the flour is incorporated and a wet, sticky dough forms.

4 Knead in the bowl until the dough is smooth and elastic, 8 to 10 minutes. Alternatively, use a silicone spatula to scoop underneath the dough and fold it in on itself repeatedly. The dough will start out maddeningly sticky; sprinkle up to 2 more tablespoons flour, just as much as needed to knead. Cover with plastic wrap or a damp dish towel and place it in the refrigerator to rise overnight. (Alternatively, you can let it rise at room temperature for 2 hours or so, until well doubled. I prefer a longer rise, to give the flavor time to develop and to split up the labor. The dough should be fine for up to 24 hours.)

5 *The next day, or at least 1 hour before baking:* Line a 9 × 5-inch Pullman loaf pan with parchment paper or grease it with butter. To make the glaze, sift the matcha powder into a medium bowl. Vigorously whisk 2 tablespoons of cream into the matcha until no lumps remain. Whisk in the remaining cream, then sift in the confectioners' sugar ¼ cup at a time, whisking after each addition, until the mixture forms a very thick, barely pourable glaze.

6 Turn the dough out onto a well-floured surface. Roll the dough out thin, thin, thin, to about an 18 × 24-inch rectangle, making sure to lift the dough and add more flour to the work surface as you go.

7 When the dough is evenly rolled out, reserve ¼ cup of the glaze and spread the rest in a very thin layer across the dough. Using a pizza cutter, sharp knife, or scissors, slice the dough in half lengthwise to form 2 long 9 × 24-inch strips. Carefully lift one strip and place it on top of the other. If desired, trim the edges into a neater rectangle, then, starting at a 9-inch end, roll the stack into a short, thick log.

8 Using a sharp, serrated knife, slice the log widthwise into 4 equal pieces. Place the rolls, cut-side down, into the loaf pan. (Things will get

(recipe continues)

messy, but do not fear. The rolls are apt to bake up a little lopsided no matter what; regardless of how they look, they all taste the same.) Let rise in a warm place until the dough is boisterously puffy and fills the pan, 1 to 1½ hours. When the dough is pressed with a finger, it should bounce back very slightly, but the indent should remain.

9 During the last half-hour of the second rise, preheat the oven to 350°F. Bake, uncovered, for 35 to 40 minutes, until golden-brown on top. Let cool, then drizzle with the remaining glaze and enjoy.

NOTES

If using instant yeast, use the same amount as active dry yeast, but mix it in with the dry ingredients instead of adding it to the scalded milk. If you can find SAF Instant Yeast, I have found it to be wonderful and reliable, with yeast goods that are fluffier, softer, and more flavorful than most.

The many thin layers and the shape of the rolls mean that this bread often bakes up a little wonky, with the swirls facing this way and that. It will all taste good, but if the appearance is frustrating you, here are a few tips and suggestions:

- To get the dough into an even rectangle with less rounded, more defined corners—which will result in a more even loaf—start by shaping the dough into a rectangle before rolling it out.

- When rolling, occasionally roll toward the corners (forming an X shape) rather than toward the sides (like a plus sign).

- After the dough has been rolled into a log, wrap it in plastic wrap and pop it into the freezer for 15 to 20 minutes, which will make slicing easier. Note, however, that this will make the second rise take longer, up to 1½ hours.

- Roll the dough into a smaller rectangle, about 8 × 16 inches, which will result in thicker layers (more similar to traditional cinnamon rolls) but a much easier time shaping and handling the rolls. You may want to use less glaze inside the dough in this case (you can save the extra for drizzling on top), as it tends to ooze out when rolled up, if used in excess.

- Shape the bread in a braided swirl pattern, as shown and described in the black sesame variation (page 238). The glaze will make it drippy and messy, but the way it bakes up in the end is beautiful.

A BLACK SESAME (LITERAL) TWIST

Makes one 9 × 5-inch loaf

The sweet dough from the previous recipe is just as good with the black sesame filling used in the Black Sesame–Stuffed French Toast (page 43). When using black sesame, I like to take advantage of the thicker paste and shape the loaf in a twisted bread technique that I learned from Sarah Kieffer of the *Vanilla Bean Blog*. You also see this method used in the chocolate krantz cake in Yotam Ottolenghi's masterpiece, *Jerusalem*. It's incredibly fun to shape, and much more forgiving in how it bakes than the sometimes cockeyed rolls for the Matcha-Glazed Swirl Bread (page 232)—no matter how you place the twist into the pan, it will bake up stunningly every time.

1 batch sweet dough (page 232), prepared to the end of the first rise

All-purpose flour, for rolling

1 batch black sesame filling for the Black Sesame–Stuffed French Toast (page 43)

1 large egg mixed with a splash of water, for egg wash

Sweetened condensed milk, for drizzling (optional)

NOTES

For a sweetened condensed milk glaze that will harden and not soak into the bread, whisk together ½ cup sweetened condensed milk with ½ cup confectioners' sugar.

---

1 Make the sweet dough up until the end of the first rise. After the dough has completed its first rise, remove it from the refrigerator and place on a generously floured work surface. Roll the dough into a roughly 14 × 18-inch rectangle and spread the filling evenly across the dough, leaving a ½-inch border around the edges.

2 Starting with the 14-inch side, roll the dough up into a tight log. You can also decide to roll a longer log using the 18-inch side—the shorter end will form more layers, the longer end more twists.

3 Using scissors or a sharp knife, gently cut the roll in half lengthwise, forming two half-moon cylinders with the layers of dough and black sesame filling visible. With the cut sides facing up, pinch the halves together at one end.

4 Lift the right half over the left half to begin a "twisting" shape, then lift the new right half over the new left half, and continue until you've twisted the entire roll. Pinch the ends together, then carefully transfer the dough into the loaf pan. If it's too long to fit, just squeeze and twist it a bit—no harm, no foul. Let rest in a warm place until the dough is boisterously puffy and fills the pan, 1 to 1½ hours. When the dough is pressed with a finger, it should bounce back very slightly, but the indent should remain.

5 During the last half-hour of the second rise, preheat the oven to 350°F. When the dough is ready, brush with egg wash, then bake for 35 to 40 minutes, until golden-brown on top. Let cool slightly, then drizzle with sweetened condensed milk, if desired, and enjoy.

MY FAVORITE CINNAMON ROLLS

Makes 8 to 10 cinnamon rolls

As the recipe title suggests, these are my ideal cinnamon rolls. They're fantastically light and pillowy, so soft and gooey with buttery cinnamon goodness that they yield instantly under a fork, and yet they aren't cake-like, but still ever-so-slightly pliant. They're made even better by a cream cheese frosting that's somewhere between the two poles of thin glaze and thick spread, pourable but in thick dollops and ribbons, not too tart but not tooth-achingly sweet. To have them in time for breakfast, make the dough or even shape the rolls a day ahead, and let them chill in the refrigerator until you're ready to bake them up in the morning.

---

1 Line a 9-inch pie dish, 10-inch cast-iron skillet, or 8-inch square baking dish with parchment paper, or butter it lightly. When the sweet dough has completed its first rise, remove it from the refrigerater and place on a generously floured work surface. Gently deflate the dough and roll it out to a 12 × 14-inch rectangle (or thereabouts), about ¼-inch thick.

2 Spread the softened butter across the dough, leaving a ½-inch border around the edges. Sprinkle the brown sugar evenly across the surface, using your fingers to gently spread it if needed, then sprinkle the cinnamon generously on top of that.

3 Roll the rectangle snugly into a log. Rolling the rectangle from the short end will give you fewer cinnamon rolls that are larger and have more swirls; rolling from the long end will yield more cinnamon rolls that are smaller and have fewer swirls. Either way you decide to go, pinch the seam shut and place the log seam-side down on a flat surface.

4 Using unflavored dental floss, fishing line, or a serrated knife, gently slice the log into 8 to 10 rolls, a little more than 1-inch wide. If using a knife, cut by gently moving the blade back and forth in a sawing motion to avoid pressing down on the dough; this should help the rolls keep their shape. It's important to use a serrated knife rather than a smooth-edged one for this reason.

(recipe continues)

FOR THE DOUGH

Butter, for the dish (optional)

1 batch sweet dough (page 232), prepared to the end of the first rise

All-purpose flour, for rolling

FOR THE FILLING

¼ cup (½ stick) unsalted butter, softened

½ cup packed light brown sugar

1 tablespoon cinnamon, or more to taste

FOR THE FROSTING

¼ cup (½ stick) unsalted butter, softened

¼ cup cream cheese, softened

1 cup confectioners' sugar

½ teaspoon vanilla extract

1 to 2 tablespoons milk of your choice, or as needed for thinning (optional)

5 Place the rolls cut-side down into the baking dish. Leave an inch or so between rolls for them to expand; if you run out of room, bake the extras in individual ramekins or free-form on a baking sheet. Cover loosely with plastic wrap or a damp dish towel and let rise until the rolls are boisterously puffy and fill the pan, about 1 hour. If you like, you can do another overnight rise in the refrigerator at this point, or even freeze the rolls, well wrapped, for later. Either way, bring the rolls to room temperature before baking.

6 About 30 minutes before you're ready to bake, preheat the oven to 350°F. When the rolls have finished rising, bake them for 20 to 22 minutes, until lightly golden on top—this will ensure that they're still nice and soft in the center. If using a cast-iron pan, you may want to take them out a minute or two earlier, since the pan retains heat very well and will continue to cook the rolls for a bit afterward.

7 While the rolls cool, make the frosting. Using an electric mixer or plenty of arm strength, beat the butter and cream cheese together until smooth. Add the confectioners' sugar in batches, beating vigorously after each addition until smooth. Finally, add the vanilla and beat again to incorporate. If you want more of a glaze than a frosting, add milk 1 tablespoon at a time, until it reaches your desired consistency (I add about 2 tablespoons total). Spread the glaze over the rolls while still slightly warm to let the frosting melt into the crags, and enjoy immediately.

NOTES
A tablespoon of maple syrup in the frosting is a favorite variation of ours; a little bourbon wouldn't hurt anything, either.

WHITE PEACH & LYCHEE CAKE

Makes one 10-inch round or one 9-inch square cake

The idea for this cake came from a white peach and lychee cobbler I made a few summers back. White peaches or nectarines are, far and away, some of my favorite fruits—unlike their yellow cousins, they're delicate, pure, and sweet, with no hint of tartness. They pair particularly well with lychee, whose heady perfume perfectly matches the dainty floral notes in the peaches. Together, when nestled underneath a blanket of buttery vanilla cake with just a hint of nutmeg, the dessert that results could not be more perfectly summery. Eating it reminds me of hot summer afternoons in Shanghai with my great-grandmother, peeling sticky lychee in the front room of her creaky townhouse, with the heat resting ponderous and lazy on our shoulders, and summer blooms reaching in through the open windows.

---

1 Preheat the oven to 350°F. Line the bottom of a 10-inch cast-iron skillet or cake round with parchment paper.

2 *Make the topping:* Place the peaches in a single layer in the bottom of the skillet. Use the lychee to fill in any gaps between the peach slices until the bottom of the skillet is evenly covered in fruit.

3 In a small saucepan or skillet, combine the sugar and water for the topping. Cook over medium heat at a steady simmer until the mixture turns amber, shiny, and viscous, about 10 minutes. Immediately remove from heat and drizzle the sugar mixture evenly over the fruit in the skillet. It will likely harden before you add the cake batter—this is fine.

4 *Make the cake:* In a medium bowl, whisk together the flour, baking powder, baking soda, nutmeg, and salt. In a liquid measuring cup or small bowl, whisk together the yogurt and milk until combined. Set both of these aside.

(recipe continues)

FOR THE TOPPING

2 to 3 ripe white peaches or nectarines, pitted and sliced (about 1½ cups)

3 to 4 tablespoons peeled, seeded, and diced lychee, fresh or canned (3 to 4 lychee)

6 tablespoons sugar

3 tablespoons water

FOR THE CAKE

1½ cups (187 grams) all-purpose flour

½ teaspoon baking powder

½ teaspoon baking soda

¼ teaspoon ground nutmeg

¼ teaspoon salt

¾ cup full-fat Greek yogurt

¼ cup whole milk

6 tablespoons (¾ stick) unsalted butter, softened

¾ cup sugar

2 large eggs

1 teaspoon vanilla extract

½ cup peeled, seeded, and diced lychee, fresh or canned (5 to 6 lychee)

FOR SERVING

Whipped cream, ice cream, or Greek yogurt

5 In a large bowl, beat together the butter and sugar until light and fluffy. Beat in the eggs, one at a time, until well combined. Whisk in the vanilla. Gently fold half the flour mixture into the butter mixture, until just barely combined (you should still see floury streaks). Fold in the yogurt-and-milk mixture, again until barely combined, followed by the remaining flour mixture and the ½ cup lychee. Mix gently to avoid over-mixing, which creates a dense cake. When all the flour has been incorporated, the batter should still be somewhat lumpy and craggy. Dollop the batter evenly over the sugar syrup and fruit and spread until smooth.

6 Bake for 30 to 35 minutes, until the top is golden brown and the cake has set. Remove from the oven and let cool. When cooled, turn the cake out onto a platter and peel off the parchment paper. Serve with whipped cream, ice cream, or more Greek yogurt on the side.

CHILLED MANGO SWEET SOUP WITH ALMOND JELLY

Serves 3 or 4

FOR THE ALMOND JELLY

1½ cups water, divided

2 (¼-ounce) envelopes powdered gelatin (about 1½ tablespoons)

1 cup whole milk or milk of your choice

½ cup sugar

2 to 3 teaspoons almond extract, or more to taste

FOR THE SOUP

2 cups cubed ripe mango (2 to 3 mangoes)

¾ cup unsweetened coconut milk, divided

½ to ¾ cup mango juice, as needed for thinning

1 tablespoon honey, if needed

1 grapefruit (or pomelo, if you can find it)

In Hong Kong you can often find versions of a dessert I love called mango pomelo sago, where juicy pomelo vesicles and sago pearls are suspended in a beguiling nectar made from puréed mango and coconut milk. My favorite version added a teetering heap of sweet tofu on top, which I've since replaced with wobbly almond jelly. If you can find pomelo, certainly use it here; if not, grapefruit provides a tangy substitute.

---

1 *To make the almond jelly:* Combine ½ cup water and the gelatin in a small bowl and let sit until the mixture forms a thick jelly, about 5 minutes. In the meantime, in a small saucepan over high heat, bring the remaining water to just shy of boiling, or heat the water in a small microwave-safe bowl in the microwave, about 1 minute. Whisk in the gelatin mixture, milk, and sugar. Add 2 teaspoons of almond extract, then taste. If the almond flavor isn't strong enough, mix in the remaining teaspoon (or more, if you like). Pour the mixture into a 9-inch square baking dish and refrigerate until firm, 4 to 6 hours. When firm, slice into ½- to 1-inch cubes and refrigerate until ready to use.

2 *To make the mango sweet soup:* In a blender or food processor, combine the mango and coconut milk and blend until smooth. Stir in the mango juice until the soup reaches your desired consistency. Taste and adjust the sweetness with honey, if necessary.

3 *To supreme the grapefruit:* Wash the grapefruit, then slice off each end so that it sits flat on the cutting board. Cut the peel away from the grapefruit, exposing the segments inside, then cut inside the membranes to remove each segment.

4 *To serve:* Divide the soup between 3 or 4 small bowls, then top with the grapefruit segments and almond jelly. Drizzle with the remaining coconut milk and enjoy.

NOTES

This dessert is traditionally served with pomelo vesicles, the tear-shaped sacs inside the fruit segments, which come apart easily and are the prettiest confetti topping on many Cantonese desserts. If you can find pomelo, it works wonderfully here, and there is no need to supreme it. Once you've removed the very thick rind, each segment's membranes can be peeled off to reveal the sacs, which should separate easily.

If you can find it or like to make it at home, the Hawaiian dessert *haupia* is another wonderful substitute for the almond jelly, and it adds an extra-coconutty note that complements the coconut milk in the mango soup.

MILK TEA RICE PUDDING
(AND REGULAR, TOO)

Serves 4 to 6

I like to think of rice pudding as the more luxurious Southern counterpart to sweet congee (page 24), an unapologetically rich and buttery version of the congee I used to load up with sugar at the breakfast table. Given my sweet-tooth tendencies, it should come as no surprise that rice pudding has always been one of my favorite desserts. Here, I've given it a little twist to take it full circle, infusing uncooked rice with tea instead of cooking it in water, then finishing it off with plenty of the traditional milk and just a pat of butter. To make it the traditional way, with cinnamon and vanilla, a second recipe follows.

MILK TEA RICE PUDDING

⅔ cup uncooked short- or medium-grain white rice

2 cups brewed strong black tea (see Notes)

1¾ cups whole milk, or more if needed, divided

⅓ cup sugar, or more to taste

¼ teaspoon salt

1 large egg

1 tablespoon unsalted butter (optional)

½ cup sweetened condensed milk, for serving

1 In a medium saucepan over medium heat, combine the rice and tea and warm until simmering. Reduce the heat to medium-low and cook, covered, until the rice is nearly done, about 20 minutes. Add 1½ cups milk, plus the sugar and salt, and continue to cook, stirring occasionally, until thick and creamy, 15 to 20 more minutes. If the pudding begins to look too thick or too dry for your liking, add more milk, ½ cup at a time, and cook until it reaches your desired consistency.

2 In a small bowl, whisk together the remaining ¼ cup milk and the egg. Add ¼ cup of the hot rice mixture to the bowl and whisk again until thoroughly combined. (This tempers the egg so that it doesn't cook when added to the rest of the rice.)

3 Stir the egg mixture into the pot and continue to cook, stirring constantly, until it reaches your desired consistency, about 2 more minutes. Stir in the butter (if using). If desired, add more sugar. Serve warm or cold, drizzled with plenty of sweetened condensed milk.

NOTES
I like to brew the tea as I would for *yuanyang* (page 265) or Hong Kong–Style Milk Tea (page 262), by simmering 4 tablespoons loose-leaf Keemun, Ceylon, or English Breakfast tea (or 4 tea bags) in 2¼ cups water for 1 minute, then reducing the heat to very low and letting it steep for another 10 minutes, until very strong and dark.

CLASSIC RICE PUDDING

1 In a medium saucepan over medium heat, combine the rice and water, and warm until simmering. Reduce the heat to medium-low and cook, covered, until the rice is nearly done, about 20 minutes. Add 1½ cups milk, plus the sugar and salt, and continue to cook, stirring occasionally, until thick and creamy, 15 to 20 more minutes. If the pudding begins to look too thick or too dry for your liking, add more milk, ½ cup at a time, and cook until it reaches your desired consistency.

2 In a small bowl, whisk together the remaining ¼ cup milk and the egg. Add ¼ cup of the hot rice mixture to the bowl and whisk again until thoroughly combined. (This tempers the egg so that it doesn't cook when added to the rest of the rice.)

3 Stir the egg mixture into the pot and continue to cook, stirring constantly, until it reaches your desired consistency, about 2 more minutes. Stir in the butter (if using), vanilla, and cinnamon. If desired, add more sugar. Serve warm or cold.

NOTES

You can also use up leftover rice for regular rice pudding: Use 2 cups cooked rice and omit the water altogether. Simmer with 1½ cups milk, ⅓ cup sugar and ¼ teaspoon salt until thick and creamy, 20 to 25 minutes. If the pudding gets too thick before the rice has softened to your liking, add more milk, ½ cup at a time, and cook until it reaches your desired consistency. Proceed with steps 2 and 3 as written above.

⅔ cup uncooked short- or medium-grain white rice

2 cups water

1¾ cups whole milk, or more if needed, divided

⅓ cup sugar, or more to taste

¼ teaspoon salt

1 large egg

1 tablespoon unsalted butter (optional)

1 teaspoon vanilla extract

½ teaspoon cinnamon

PEANUT BUTTER MOCHI CAKE

Makes one 8-inch square cake

This easy, demure little cake was inspired by the variety of Chinese sticky soup dumplings, or *tangyuan*, that are filled with a sweet, creamy peanut filling. Dolloping the peanut butter filling across the batter of the simplest one-bowl cake, instead of rolling it up into dumplings, gives you all the satisfying chewy-sticky flavor of peanut *tangyuan* with none of the fuss. Best of all, it leaves the door open for endless variations. Replace the peanut butter filling with rich, inky black sesame (page 43), lotus, or red bean pastes, go a totally untraditional route and add chocolate chips, or swirl in some jelly for a PB&J mochi cake—it's all delicious.

6 tablespoons peanut butter (smooth or crunchy)

2 tablespoons confectioners' sugar

1½ cups (225 grams) sweet rice flour, like Mochiko Blue Star

1 cup whole milk

¾ cup sugar

½ cup vegetable oil or other neutral oil

2 large eggs

1 teaspoon vanilla extract

½ cup roasted peanuts

1 Preheat the oven to 350°F and line an 8-inch square baking dish with parchment paper. In a small bowl, whisk together the peanut butter and confectioners' sugar until smooth. Set aside.

2 In a medium bowl, combine the sweet rice flour, milk, sugar, oil, eggs, and vanilla, and whisk until smooth. You don't need to worry about overworking the batter and making the cake dense, because sweet rice flour doesn't contain gluten—mochi cake is dense to begin with! Small lumps will appear in the batter at first, but they will dissipate as you whisk.

3 Pour half the batter into the prepared baking dish. Drop small spoonfuls of the peanut butter filling evenly across the batter, then pour the remaining batter over the peanut butter filling. Bake, uncovered, for 20 minutes.

4 While the mochi is baking, place the peanuts in a food processor or blender and pulse until crumbly. Remove the mochi from the oven, sprinkle the crushed peanuts across the top, then return the cake to the oven and bake until the center bounces back when pressed, an additional 15 to 20 minutes. Enjoy warm or at room temperature. The mochi will slice much more cleanly when cooled, but there's nothing like enjoying a piece warm from the oven.

DRINKS

GINGER-CINNAMON PUNCH
(SUJEONGGWA)

Serves 6 to 8

Whenever this ice-cold, jewel-toned punch appears as the after-dinner treat at a Korean restaurant, I always end up collecting all the untouched cups from those who didn't want theirs after I've downed mine. Ticklingly warm from the cinnamon and spicy from the ginger, yet crisp and cold, it is a play in contrasts that is utterly addictive and so very easy to make at home. Brew up a hefty batch and store in the fridge to sip at your leisure—no need to poach from your dinner companions.

Combine the ginger, cinnamon, and water in a large saucepan. Bring to a simmer over high heat, then reduce to medium-low and simmer gently until the tea turns a rich red, 30 to 40 minutes. Add the sugar and continue to simmer for another 5 minutes or so, stirring occasionally, until the sugar is fully dissolved. Strain the tea through a coffee filter or layers of cheesecloth to remove any residue. Refrigerate until very cold. Enjoy chilled, with a few pine nuts and a slice of dried persimmon, or a handful of dried apricots or dates, if desired. The tea will keep for up to a week in the refrigerator.

4 inches ginger root, sliced (scant ⅓ cup, or 1 ounce)

9 or 10 cinnamon sticks (about 1 ounce)

8 cups water

1 cup sugar

¼ cup pine nuts

Dried persimmons, apricots, or dates (optional)

SWEET TEA

Serves 4; easily doubled

4 cups water

1 family-size Luzianne tea bag, or 4 regular tea bags (Lipton works in a pinch)

¼ to ½ cup sugar, to taste

⅛ teaspoon baking soda (optional)

The first time I ate at a restaurant in New York, the server came by to take our drink orders. "Sweet tea, please," I answered automatically, and a few moments passed before I realized that my order was met, not with a tall, frosty glass of syrupy-sweet amber tea, but a blank stare.

In the South, unlike most of the rest of the country, sweet tea graces tables more frequently than water. The tea is brewed nice and strong to stand up to more shimmering sugar than should be prudent or even possible, with just a pinch of baking soda to cut any astringency, and poured over a tall glass stacked high with ice. Having since moved to strange lands where sweet tea is a novelty and not a natural part of life, I've taken to brewing it at home whenever I feel a pang of homesickness (or a craving for sugar). Luzianne is the traditional choice if you can find it, but Lipton will do just fine if that's all you have.

Bring the water to a rolling boil, then remove from the heat and add the tea bags. Let steep for 8 to 10 minutes, until strong. Remove the bags and stir in the sugar. Taste and adjust the sugar to your liking. It is meant to be quite sweet (hence the name!) so don't shy away from the sugar—it will also be served over ice, so it won't be quite as concentrated as it tastes right now. If the tea is a little bitter, add the baking soda. Let cool completely, then pour over ice and enjoy, or store in the refrigerator for 3 to 4 days.

NOTES

To enjoy more quickly, steep the tea in 2 cups boiling water instead of 4 cups. Remove the tea bags, stir in the sugar and baking soda until dissolved, then stir in 2 more cups ice-cold water. Pour over ice and enjoy.

For a milder tea, use just 3 regular tea bags, or steep the tea for less time, instead (6 to 8 minutes).

WHITE PEACH GREEN TEA

Serves 3 or 4

I'm not much of a sangria drinker, but whenever the summer rolls around and frosty pitchers adorn all the restaurant patios, heavy with fruit, I always wish I was. This is my simple, alcohol-free solution—a summer tea that matches pure, delicate white peaches with the crisp grassiness of green tea for a light, fresh alternative to regular Sweet Tea (page 258) or sangria. Replace the green tea with jasmine for a more tea-forward, floral alternative, or with black tea if you prefer it, or any other favorite.

FOR THE PEACH SYRUP (OPTIONAL, SEE NOTES)

½ cup water

⅓ to ½ cup sugar or honey

1 to 2 ripe white peaches or nectarines, sliced into chunks (about ½ cup)

FOR THE TEA

2 to 3 tablespoons loose-leaf green tea, or 3 or 4 tea bags

1 quart water

1 ripe white peach or nectarine, sliced

---

1 *Make the peach syrup:* In a small saucepan, combine the water, sugar (or honey), and peaches and bring to a boil over medium-high heat, stirring occasionally. Reduce the heat to low and let simmer until the peaches are very soft, 10 to 15 minutes. Use a wooden spoon to crush the peaches against the sides of the saucepan to release more flavor. Set aside and let cool completely.

2 *Meanwhile, make the tea:* Place the green tea in a pitcher. Bring the water to a boil, then remove from the heat and let cool briefly, about 10 seconds or so. Pour over the green tea and let steep 3 to 4 minutes. Strain out the tea and let cool.

3 Divide the remaining sliced peach between 3 or 4 glasses and muddle if desired. Strain out the peaches from the syrup and add the syrup to the green tea until it reaches your desired sweetness. Pour over the muddled peaches and plenty of ice, and serve.

NOTES

For a lighter, more natural tea, simply muddle the peaches, pour the hot tea over it, and let cool before enjoying.

MILK TEA, TWO WAYS

Serves 2 or 3

While I learned quickly that the strong, smoky milk tea in Hong Kong was made by steeping black tea until inky and then stirring in creamy evaporated milk or thick ribbons of condensed milk, for the longest time I didn't know how Taiwanese bubble tea chains got their milk tea to taste so distinctive. Try as I might to combine evaporated milk with sweetened condensed milk or regular milk, it never tasted quite the same. Finally, I picked up the phone to ask them myself, steeling myself for a shut-down. Surely it was a trade secret that they'd refuse to share? But instead, I got the answer right away. "Powdered nondairy creamer," was the curt answer. I received the same reply from the next bubble tea chain I called, and the next. Really? Incredulous, I went out and bought a dubious-looking container of the stuff. The moment I stirred it in—there it was.

These days I love both recipes, though I prefer my Hong Kong–style milk tea hot and my Taiwanese-style milk tea cold, with bubbles. Whichever one you prefer, steep the tea until it's nice and strong, and don't hold back with the bells and whistles—the creamy sweetness is what you're here for.

HONG KONG-STYLE

2 cups water

4 tablespoons loose-leaf Keemun, Ceylon, or English Breakfast tea, or 4 tea bags

⅛ teaspoon baking soda

¼ to ½ cup evaporated milk (and/or sweetened condensed milk), to taste

2 to 4 tablespoons sugar, to taste

1 In a small saucepan over medium-high heat, bring the water to a boil. Reduce the heat to medium, add the tea, and simmer for 1 minute. (If using tea bags, snip off the strings and tags before adding.) Reduce the heat to its very lowest setting and let steep until the tea is very dark and strong, about 10 more minutes. Strain out the tea leaves, add the baking soda, then divide the tea between 2 or 3 cups.

2 Stir in 2 to 3 tablespoons evaporated milk per cup, and about 1 tablespoon sugar per cup (or more or less, depending on your preference). Alternatively, use 1 to 2 tablespoons sweetened condensed milk plus 1 to 2 tablespoons evaporated milk per cup, and omit or reduce the sugar. Enjoy hot or cold.

(recipe continues)

NOTES

Because sweetened condensed milk and evaporated milk are quite creamy, I prefer Hong Kong–style milk tea when it is, by traditional standards, intentionally over-brewed. For my tastes, the milk and baking soda are more than enough to smooth out any astringency, but if you like your tea a bit smoother, place the tea in a teapot, bring the water to a boil separately in a small saucepan or kettle, then pour the water over the tea. Let steep for a bit longer than you would for your normal cup of tea, until dark and extra strong (6 to 8 minutes), then enjoy.

TAIWANESE-STYLE

FOR THE BUBBLES

2 cups water

¼ cup black tapioca pearls (I like Wu Fu Yuan brand)

1 tablespoon dark brown sugar, or to taste

FOR THE TEA

4 tablespoons loose-leaf Keemun, Ceylon, or English Breakfast tea, or 4 tea bags

2 cups water

3 to 4 tablespoons powdered nondairy creamer, to taste

2 to 4 tablespoons sugar, to taste

⅛ teaspoon baking soda

1 *Make the bubbles:* In a small saucepan over high heat, bring the water to a boil. Add the pearls and stir gently so that they don't clump together. Wait for the pearls to float to the surface, then cover, reduce the heat to medium, and simmer for 2 to 3 minutes. Turn off the heat and let sit for another 1 to 3 minutes, depending on how firm you like your bubbles (I find that 1 minute is enough). Drain the pot, then submerge the bubbles in cold water until cool to the touch. Drain again, stir in a tablespoon or so of brown sugar, and divide between 2 or 3 cups. Set aside.

2 *Make the tea:* Place the tea in a teapot or liquid measuring cup. Rinse out the saucepan, then add 2 cups water and bring to a boil. Pour the boiling water over the tea and let steep until strong and dark, 6 to 7 minutes. Add powdered nondairy creamer and sugar to taste. Stir in the baking soda, then divide between the 2 or 3 cups if enjoying hot; if you'd like it cold, let it cool briefly, then add ice to the cups and pour the tea on top.

HONG KONG COFFEE TEA
(YUANYANG)

Serves 2 to 4

Yuanyang is one of those truly remarkable combinations that creates something wholly new out of two things that you'd never think would go together. Made from two parts tea and one part coffee, it manages to taste nothing like tea *or* coffee, but becomes a smoky, earthy, alluring morning wake-up all its own. Enjoy it with a soft scrambled egg sandwich or sweetened condensed milk and peanut butter toast (page 37), for a luxurious Hong Kong–style way to start the day.

2 cups water

¼ cup loose-leaf Keemun, Ceylon, or English Breakfast tea, or 4 tea bags

⅛ teaspoon baking soda

1 cup strong coffee, hot

¼ to ½ cup evaporated milk (and/or sweetened condensed milk)

Sugar, to taste

1 In a small saucepan over medium-high heat, bring the water to a boil. Reduce the heat to medium, add the tea, and simmer for 1 minute. Reduce the heat to its very lowest setting and let steep until the tea is very dark and strong, about 10 more minutes. The stronger the tea, the better it will hold up to the coffee and evaporated milk. Stir in the baking soda, then the coffee.

2 Divide the yuanyang between 2 to 4 cups. Stir in 2 to 3 tablespoons evaporated milk and 2 to 3 teaspoons sugar per cup (or more or less, depending on personal preference). Alternatively, use 1 to 2 tablespoons sweetened condensed milk plus 1 to 2 tablespoons evaporated milk per cup, and omit or reduce the sugar. Serve hot or cold.

HONEYDEW BUBBLE TEA

Serves 3 or 4

The first honeydew bubble tea I ever had was the sort made from effervescently green powder, scooped out of a little plastic drawer and shaken vigorously with ice to become a mysteriously composed but utterly delicious fruity-yet-creamy bubble tea. I suspect many versions out there are made in similar fashion, but with ripe honeydew melons at my disposal one summer I thought I'd see if there wasn't a better way. Lo and behold, there is—all you need is fresh, nectar-like honeydew juice, a smattering of creamy matcha, and chewy bubbles to make it happen.

---

1 Add the honeydew to a food processor or blender and blend to a purée (it should have the consistency of applesauce). Place a fine-mesh sieve over a large bowl and pour the purée into the sieve, straining the juice into the bowl. You should have about 3 to 4 cups of juice. Set aside.

2 In a small bowl, whisk together the hot water, powdered creamer, and matcha powder until no lumps remain. You may want to use a matcha whisk, if you have one. If you don't and lumps persist, strain them through a fine-mesh sieve. Depending on the sweetness of your melon, add sugar as desired and whisk again until dissolved. Combine the matcha mixture with the honeydew juice, and set aside to let cool completely.

3 To make the bubbles, in a small saucepan, bring 4 cups water to a boil over high heat. Add the pearls and stir gently so they don't clump together. Wait for the pearls to float to the surface, then reduce the heat to medium, cover, and let simmer for 2 to 3 minutes. Turn off the heat and let sit for another 1 to 3 minutes, depending on how firm you like your bubbles (I find that 1 minute is enough). Drain the pot, then submerge the bubbles in cold water until cool to the touch. Drain again, stir in 1 to 2 tablespoons sugar, and divide between 3 or 4 drinking glasses. Add a few cubes of ice to each glass, then pour the honeydew tea mixture over, and enjoy.

NOTES

If you don't have matcha powder, add a few ounces of strong green tea. You can also use jasmine tea, for a floral twist.

FOR THE TEA

1 honeydew melon, diced (about 8 cups)

¼ cup hot water

¼ to ⅓ cup powdered nondairy creamer or milk of your choice, to taste

2 teaspoons matcha powder, or to taste (see Notes)

1 to 2 tablespoons sugar, if needed

FOR THE BUBBLES

½ cup black tapioca pearls (I like Wu Fu Yuan brand)

4 cups water

1 to 2 tablespoons sugar, to taste

MATCHA HOT CHOCOLATE

Serves 2 or 3

2 cups milk of your choice, divided

1 tablespoon matcha powder

1 teaspoon cornstarch (optional)

3 to 4 ounces white chocolate

⅛ teaspoon salt

Marshmallows and Almond Whipped Cream (recipe follows), for serving (optional)

White chocolate seems to have a tough break of it most of the time. But while its assertive sweetness might not work in every context, I can think of no better way to use it than with matcha powder, where it becomes the perfect backdrop to the creamy, sweet notes inherent in matcha. A restrained amount of white chocolate, melted together with plenty of matcha and steamed milk until silky and thick, makes for a rich and decadent hot faux-cocoa that tastes like a particularly sassy green tea latte.

---

1 Add ¼ cup milk to a 2-quart saucepan and bring just to a simmer over medium-low heat. Remove from the heat and add the matcha powder and cornstarch (if using). Whisk vigorously to break up any lumps, then return to the heat.

2 Add the remaining 1¾ cups milk, the white chocolate, and the salt, and stir until melted. Continue to stir until the mixture just reaches a simmer, then immediately remove from the heat. Serve with plenty of marshmallows and almond whipped cream, if desired.

NOTES

For a more mild hot chocolate, use 2 teaspoons matcha powder; for a less sweet hot chocolate, use 3 ounces white chocolate. Any kind of milk will work here—I particularly like soy milk, but regular dairy is also wonderful.

---

almond whipped cream

MAKES ABOUT 2 CUPS

1 cup heavy cream, very cold

2 to 3 teaspoons sugar, or more to taste

½ teaspoon almond extract

Using an electric handheld mixer or a stand mixer, beat the heavy cream on high until soft peaks form. Add the sugar and almond extract and continue to beat on medium until the cream reaches stiff peaks. Use immediately.

NOTES

Cream will whip most readily when everything is thoroughly chilled—I like to chill the cream, the bowl, and even the mixing beaters.

CONVERSIONS

GENERAL

1 inch = 2.5 centimeters

1 pound = 16 ounces = 450 grams

1 cup = 8 fluid ounces = 237 milliliters

2 tablespoons = 1 ounce = ⅛ cup

FLOUR

1 cup all-purpose flour = 125 grams

1 cup bread flour = 128 grams

1 cup cake flour = 120 grams

1 cup cornmeal = 150 grams

1 cup cornstarch = 128 grams

1 cup sweet rice flour = 140 grams

SUGARS

1 cup granulated sugar = 200 grams

1 cup light or dark brown sugar, packed = 200 grams

1 cup confectioners' sugar = 120 grams

1 cup honey = 240 milliliters

DAIRY

1 cup milk = 227 milliliters

1 cup sweetened condensed milk = 312 milliliters

1 cup evaporated milk = 256 milliliters

1 cup cream cheese = 227 grams

1 cup plain Greek yogurt = 227 grams

EGGS (FROM *COOK'S ILLUSTRATED*)

1 large egg = 1.73 ounces = 50 grams

1 large egg white = 1.19 ounces = 34 grams

1 large egg yolk = .54 ounce = 15 grams

FATS

1 cup butter = 226 grams = 2 sticks

1 cup vegetable oil = 198 grams

1 cup mayonnaise = 226 grams

TEMPERATURES

275°F = 140°C = gas mark 1

300°F = 150°C = gas mark 2

325°F = 165°C = gas mark 3

350°F = 180°C = gas mark 4

375°F = 190°C = gas mark 5

400°F = 200°C = gas mark 6

425°F = 220°C = gas mark 7

450°F = 230°C = gas mark 9

475°F = 240°C = gas mark 10

RESOURCES

AKIKO'S POTTERY
akikospottery.com
Beautiful handmade ceramics,
our very favorites.

AMBATALIA
ambatalia.com
Kitchen linens, furoshiki,
bento bags.

ATELIER ST. GEORGE
atelierstgeorge.com
Handmade ceramics.

**ATLANTIC FRUITS &
VEGETABLES**
181 Atlantic Ave.
Brooklyn, NY 11201
Quality produce at affordable
prices—one of the stores
I miss most in Brooklyn.

**COLLEEN HENNESSEY
CLAYWORKS**
colleenhennessey.net
Handmade ceramics.

FISH TALES
191A Court St.
Brooklyn, NY 11201
High-quality fresh
seafood, a good source
for sushi-grade fish.

FOOD52
food52.com
A community-based
resource for recipes, cooking
tips, kitchen equipment,
cookbooks, and more.

GALLERIA MARKET
3250 W. Olympic Blvd.
Los Angeles, CA 90006
Supermarket specializing
in Korean ingredients.

HANNAM CHAIN
2740 W. Olympic Blvd.
Los Angeles, CA 90006
(and other locations)
Supermarket specializing
in Korean ingredients.

KING ARTHUR FLOUR
kingarthurflour.com
Flours, specialty baking
ingredients, recipes, and
baking tips.

99 RANCH
6450 Sepulveda Blvd.
Van Nuys, CA 91411
(and other locations)
Supermarket specializing
in Chinese ingredients.

NUTS.COM
nuts.com
Great dates, dried fruit,
flours, and, you guessed
it, nuts.

SAHADI'S
187 Atlantic Ave.
Brooklyn, NY 11201
Bulk spices, nuts, dried
fruits, gigantic slabs of
chocolate.

SHOP FOG LINEN
shop-foglinen.com
Kitchen linens and more.

SPECK & STONE
speckandstone.com
Handmade ceramics.

VERMONT CREAMERY
vermontcreamery.com
Cheese, cultured butter,
crème fraîche.

THANK YOU

To Andrew, my "Bowl #2," where do I begin? Thank you for being the first (and, for many months, the only) reader of *Two Red Bowls,* my biggest champion, my dinner date at meals both delicious and questionable, my compass through this wild and wonderful journey, whose stalwart, unwavering belief in me and in this book has been far more than I deserve. Thank you for reminding me that there was once a girl who found joy in creating things, who liked *Ocarina of Time* and stories set a long time ago in a galaxy far, far away, and for helping me to become her again. Without you I would have never discovered I had anything like a food blog, let alone a cookbook, inside me; you make me better, you make life brighter, and you are the best father I could have ever imagined for our baby boy. How astonishingly lucky I am to share this dinner table, and this life, with you.

To my parents, Nianyi and Wen Chen, for being the very first to instill in me that food is one of the greatest kinds of love, for a lifetime of fond food memories, and for the knowledge that wherever I make my home, I will always have my first home waiting for me—with delicious food on the table, too.

To my mother- and father-in-law, Young Mi and Patrick McTernan, for opening your hearts, your home, and your kitchen to me, making me feel so much a part of your family from the first day I met you, and for being the best second parents I could have ever asked for. If only everyone could be so fortunate to have in-laws like you!

To my wonderful friends and family for your excitement, enthusiasm, and honest opinions, especially my brother, Jeremy, and my sister-in-law, Tiffany; Aunt Maryanne and Uncle Tim, for testing recipes and cheering me on with frank, steadfast New Yorker optimism; Samantha Jaeger and A. J. Sedgewick, for making my recipes better than I can; and Katie Weiss, for taking blog leftovers off my hands since the very beginning, and so very charitably acting like it was a gift and never a burden.

A million thanks to the truly selfless, generous souls who devoted incredible time and effort to testing recipes for this book, and the many more who volunteered: Eve Jenkins, Patricia Peck, and Claire Schultz, who together tested half of the book's recipes; Sis Adger, Ben Anderson, Sacha Burn, Robin Deem, Alina Gatowski, Margaret Hunt, Connie Jew, Becky Jones, Stephanie Lau, Janet Lee, Lydia Melamedas, Danell Norby, Corinne Pickett, Christine Pince, Kelsey Reinhard, Alison Rost, Lyndsay Sung, Ruth Mar Tam, and Karen Wong.

To my agent, Judy Linden, who shepherded this clueless sheep through the cookbook process from start to finish with unfailing warmth, encouragement, and patience, and Dervla Kelly, Rae Ann Spitzenberger, Anna Cooperberg, and the entire team at Rodale and Crown, for taking a chance on this book and making it a reality.

Most of all, thank you to the readers of *Two Red Bowls,* for stumbling on that obscure corner of the Internet and, for some reason, deciding to stay—you made that corner home for me, and none of this would have been possible without you.

INDEX

ABOUT THE AUTHOR

CYNTHIA CHEN MCTERNAN is a lawyer and the self-taught home cook and photographer behind *Two Red Bowls*, a *Saveur* Blog Award winner. She graduated from Harvard Law School in 2013 and spent three years at a law firm in Manhattan before moving to Los Angeles, California, where she continues to practice law—when not cooking—and where she lives with her husband, the patient taste tester and the original owner of the two red bowls, and their baby, Luke.